Our Europe

Arya Bàhram

Our Europe

Arya Bàhram

Our Europe

Dedicate to Bee gees
Kings of Pop music with love

Arya Bàhram

Our Europe

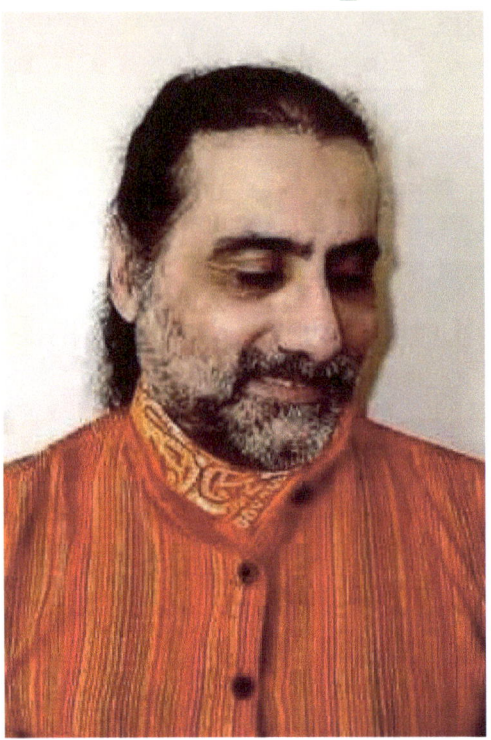

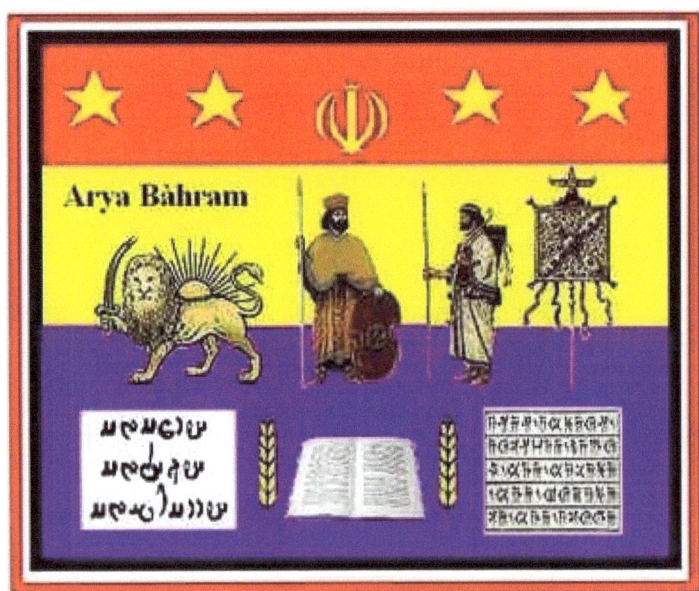

Musics for book - musiques pour livre - Musiken für Buch – آهنگها برای کتاب - Ahàng ha bàraye nibig ha

http://www.majidbahrambeiguy.at/my-foto-books---mes-livres-des-photos-.html

Arya Bàhram

Our Europe

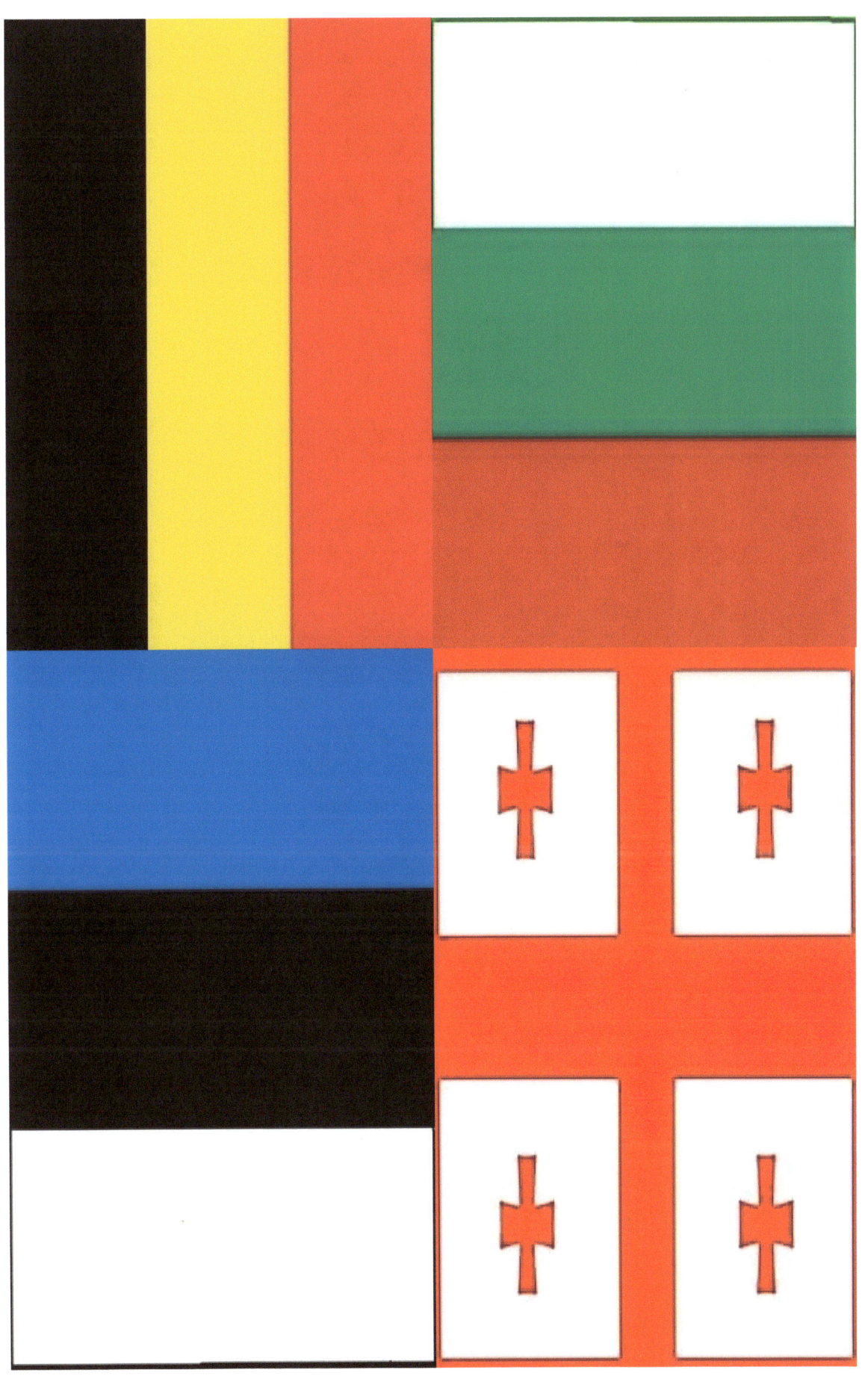

Arya Bàhram

Our Europe

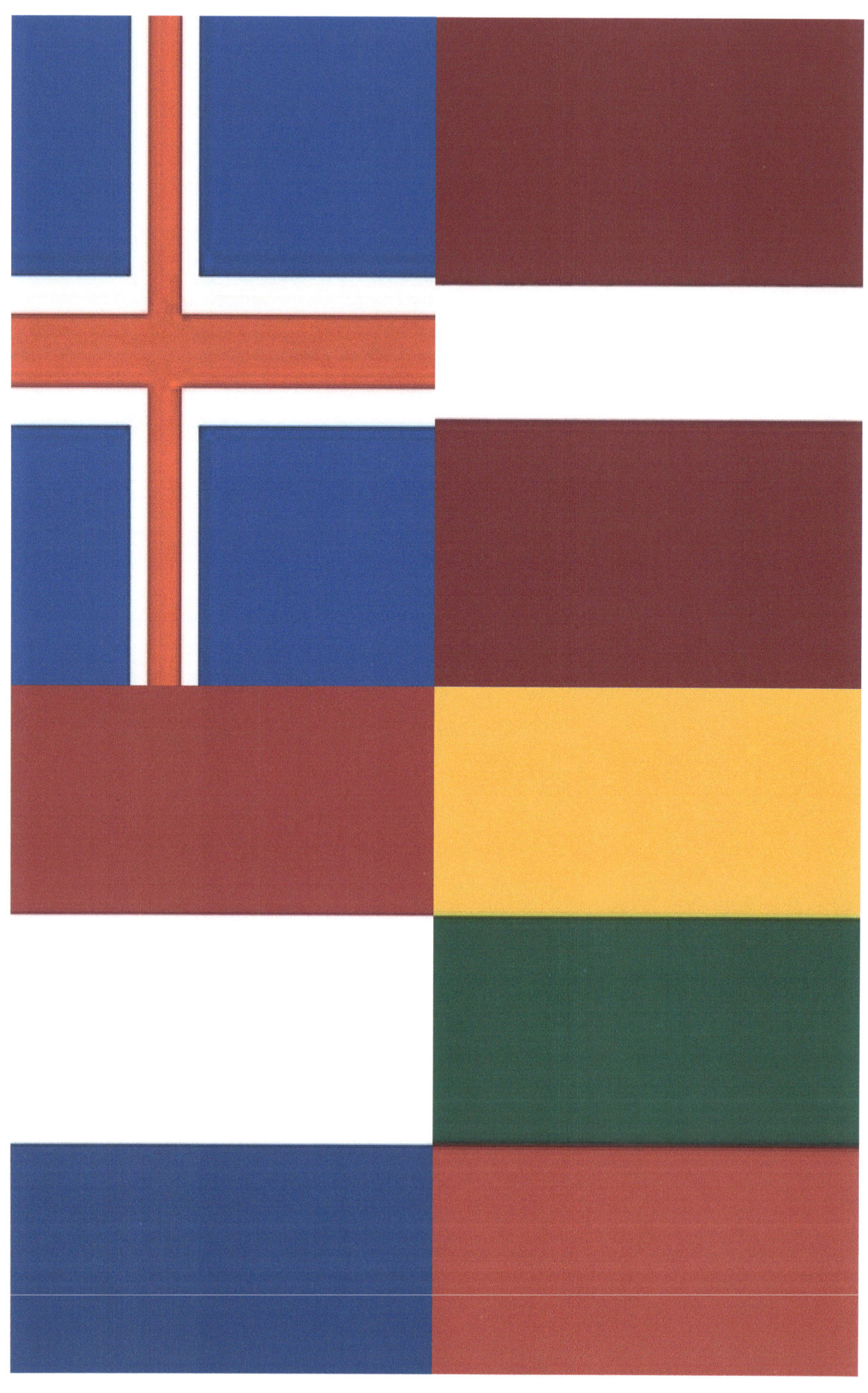

Arya Bàhram

Our Europe

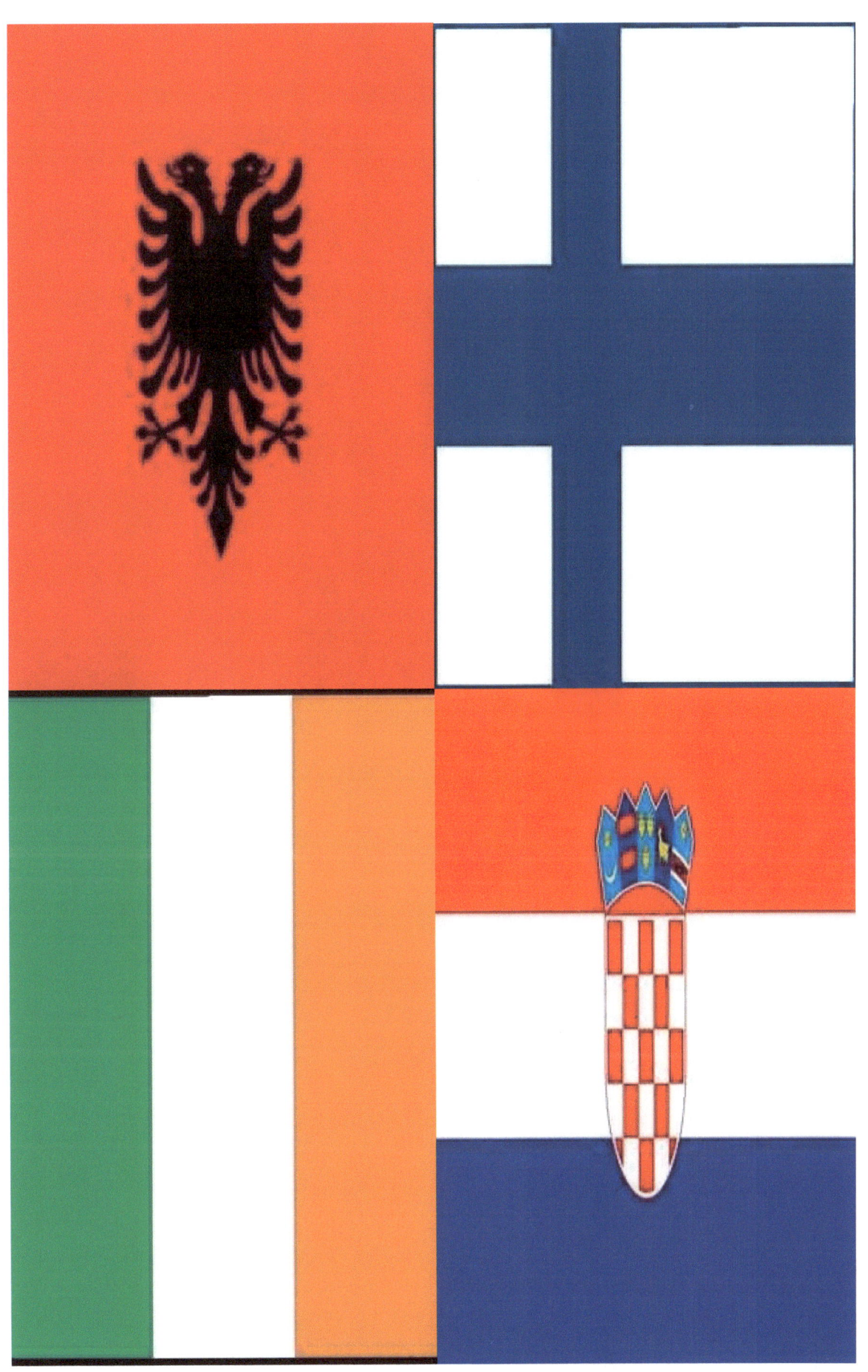

Arya Bàhram

Our Europe

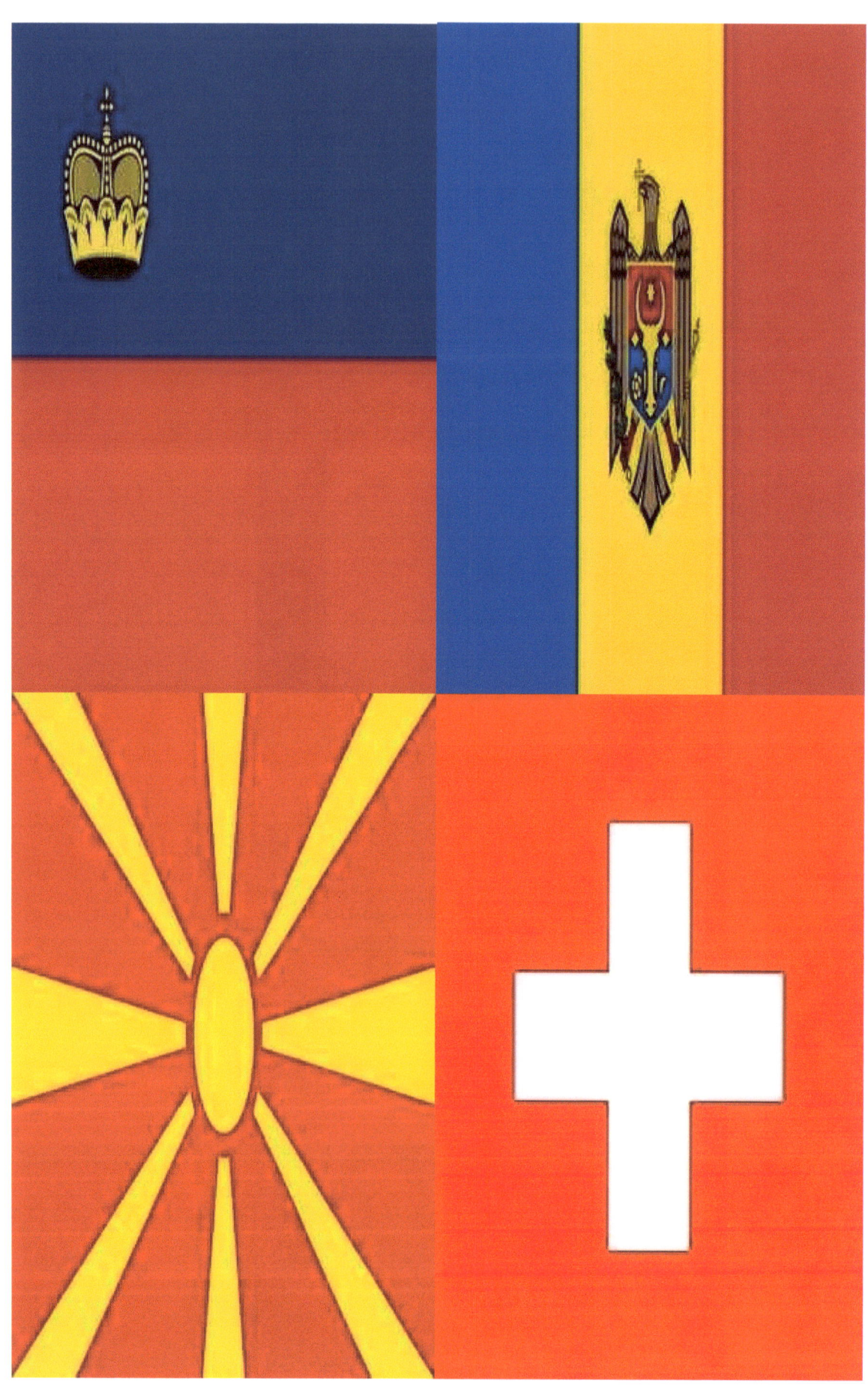

Arya Bàhram

Our Europe

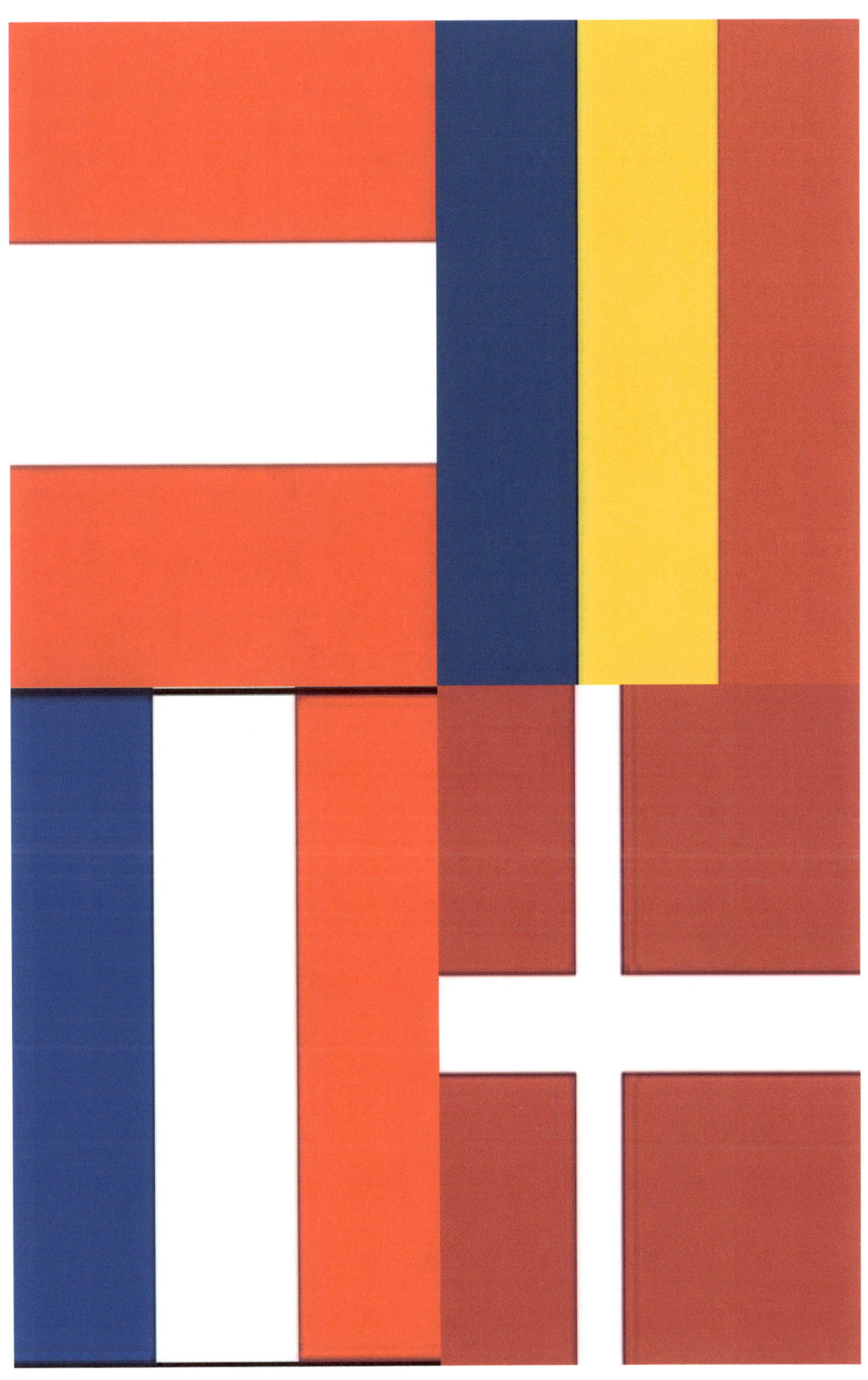

Arya Bàhram

Our Europe

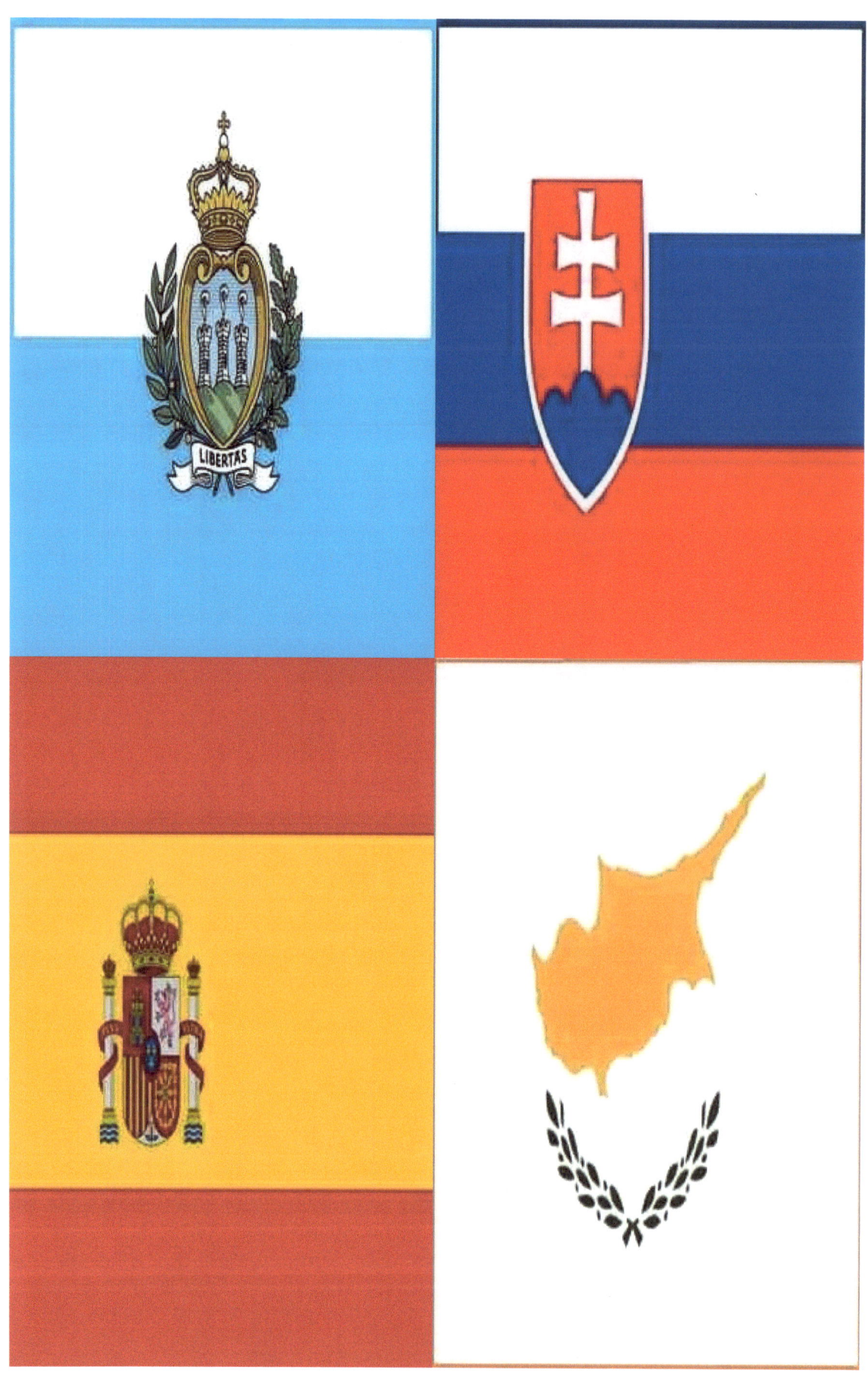

Arya Bàhram

Our Europe

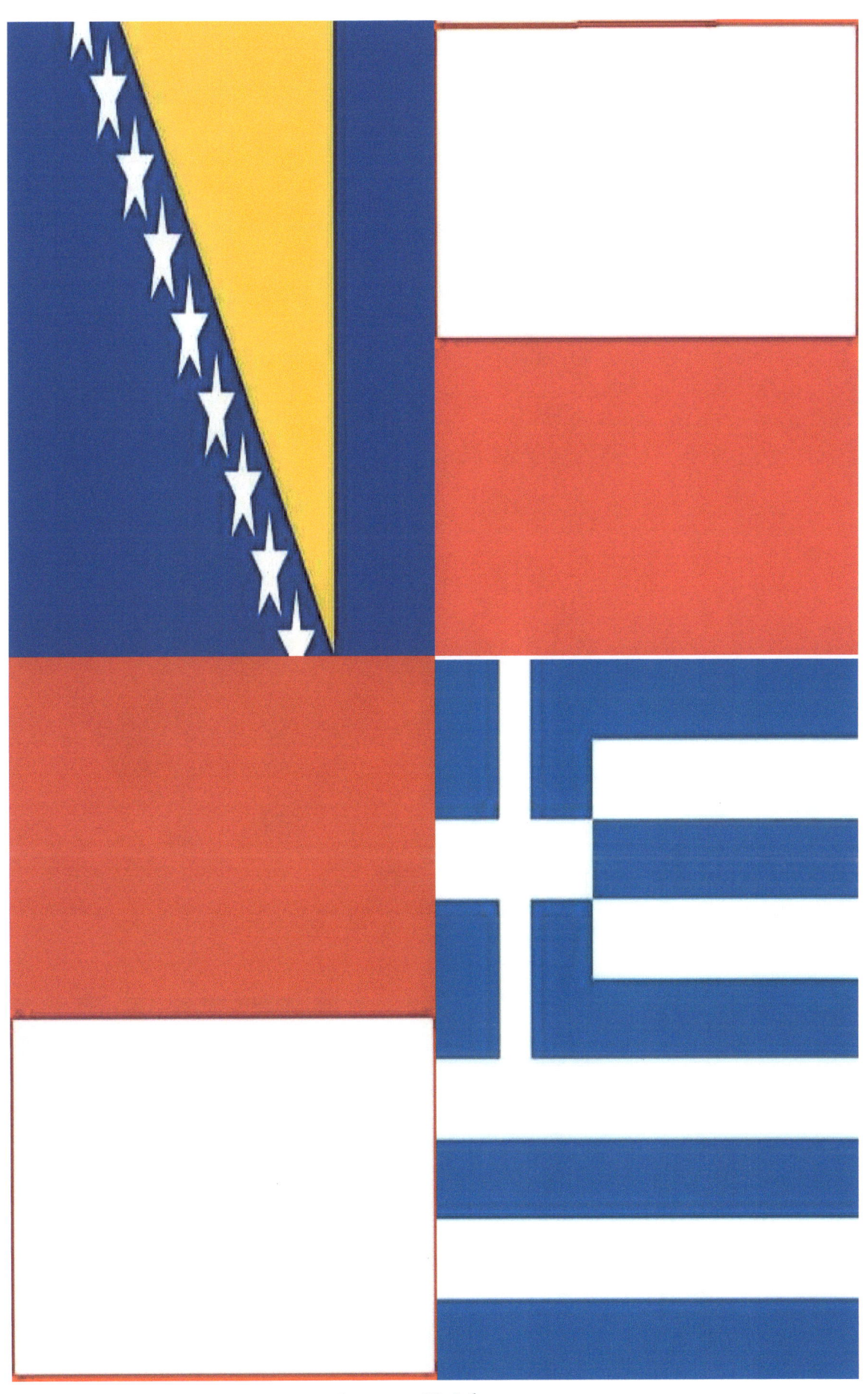

Arya Bàhram

Our Europe

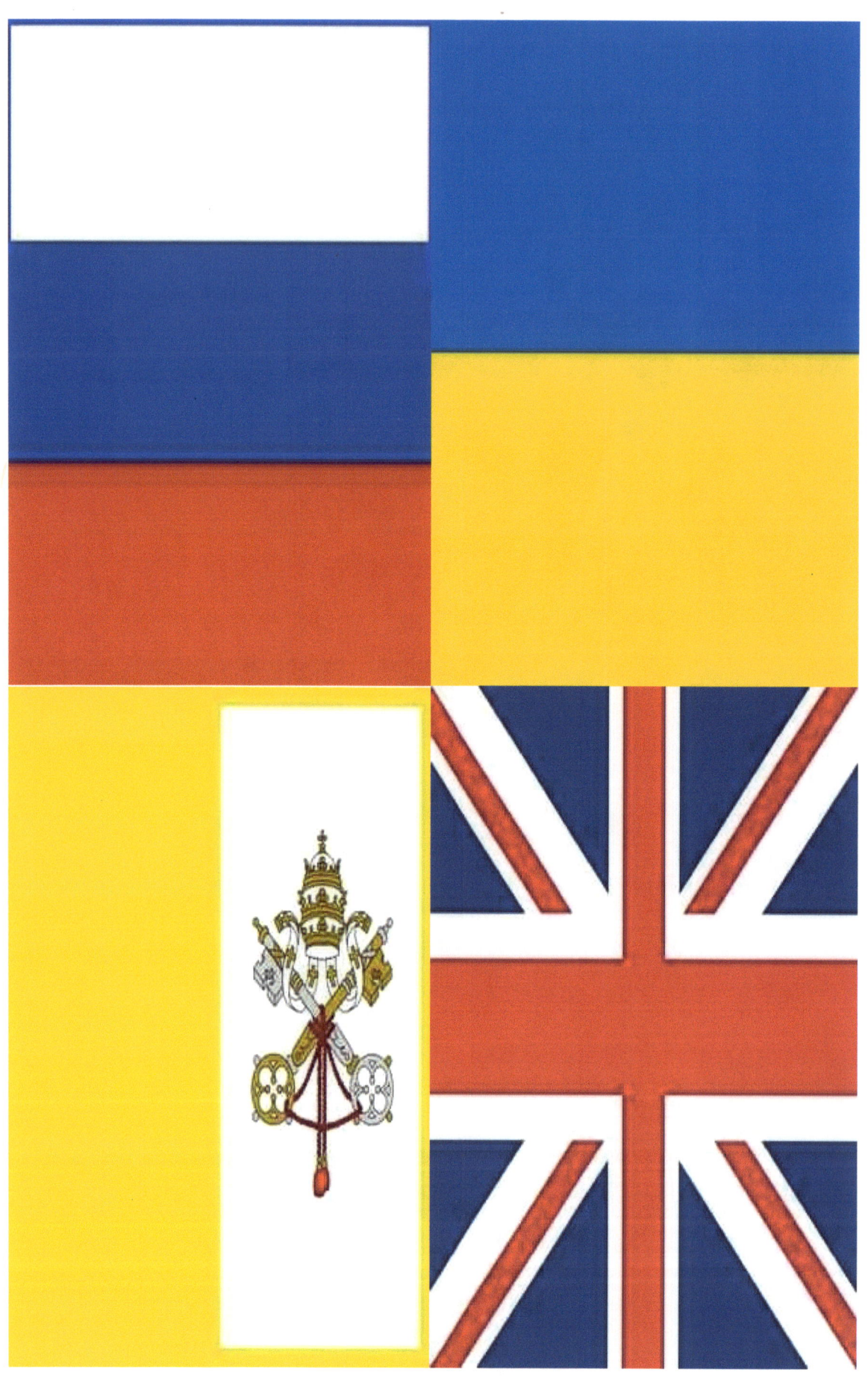

Arya Bàhram

Our Europe

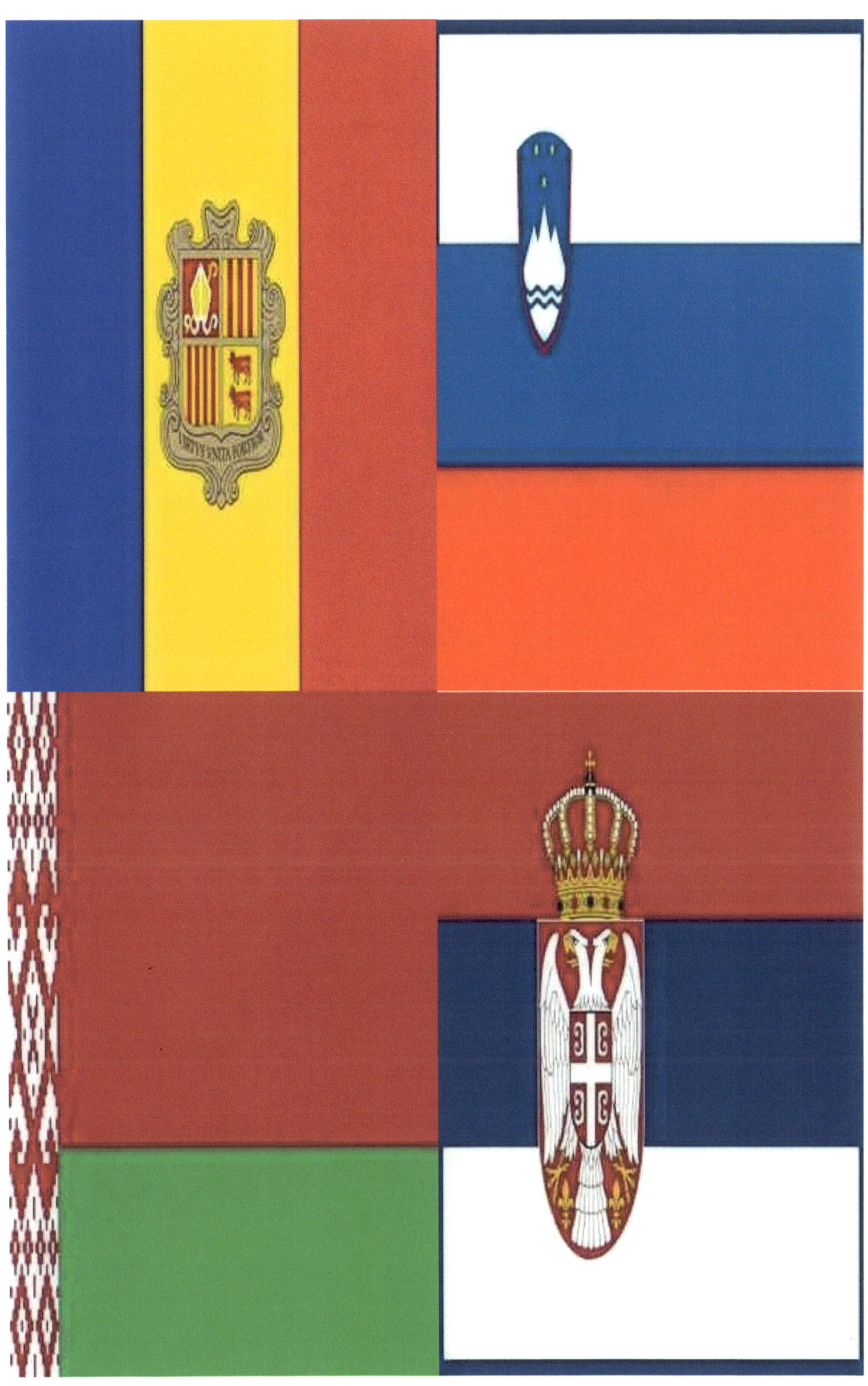

Arya Bàhram

Our Europe

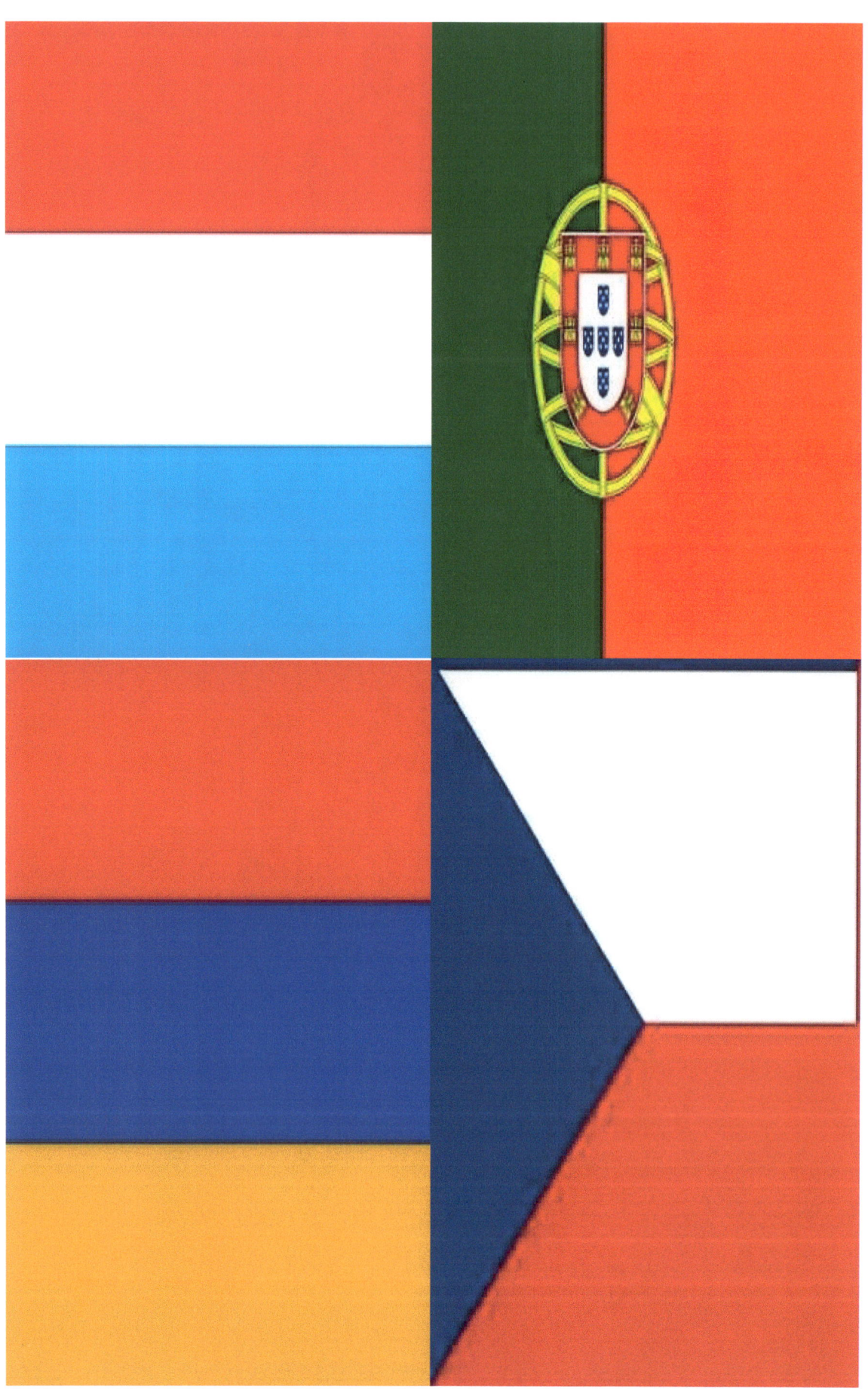

Arya Bàhram

Our Europe

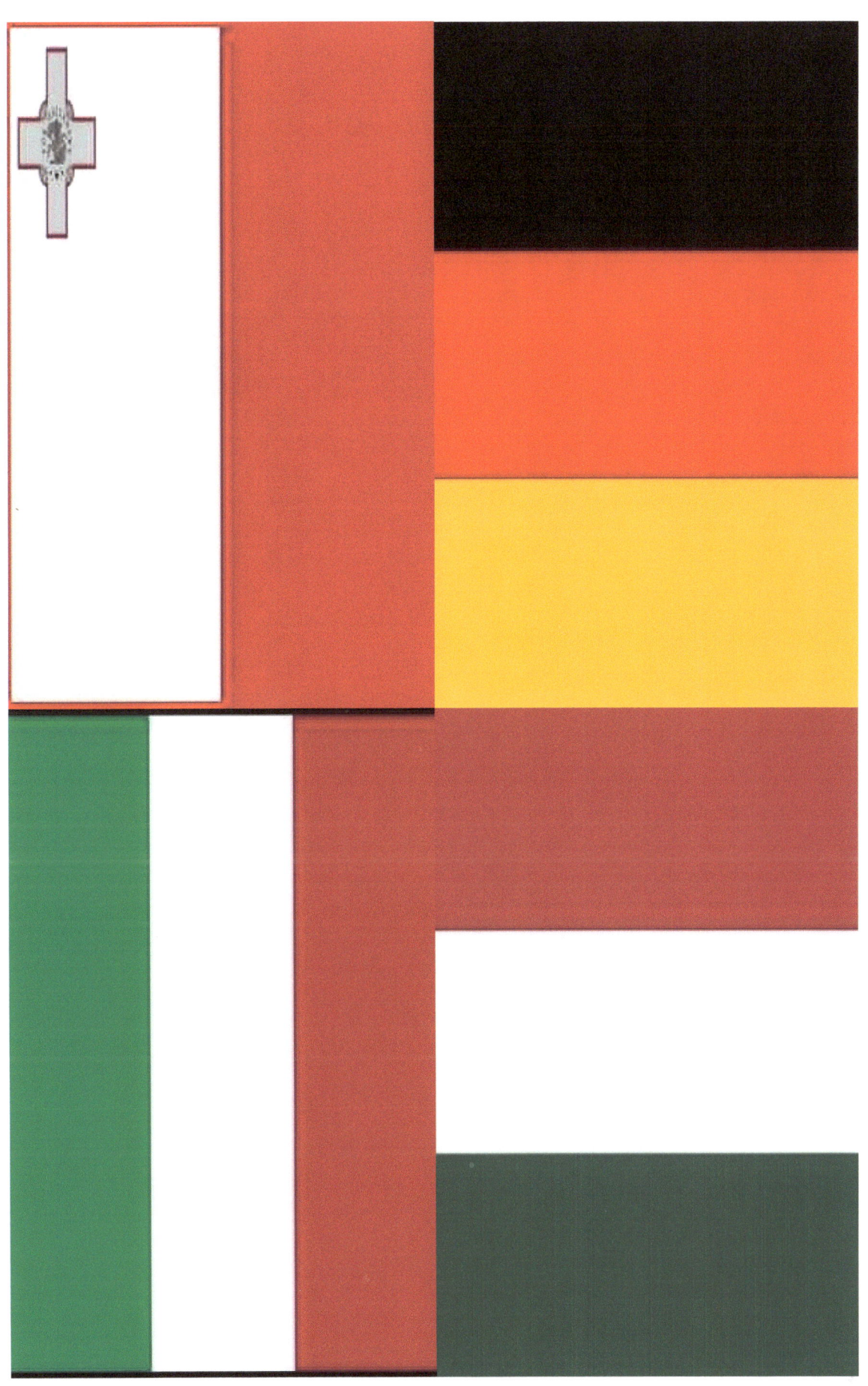

Arya Bàhram

Our Europe

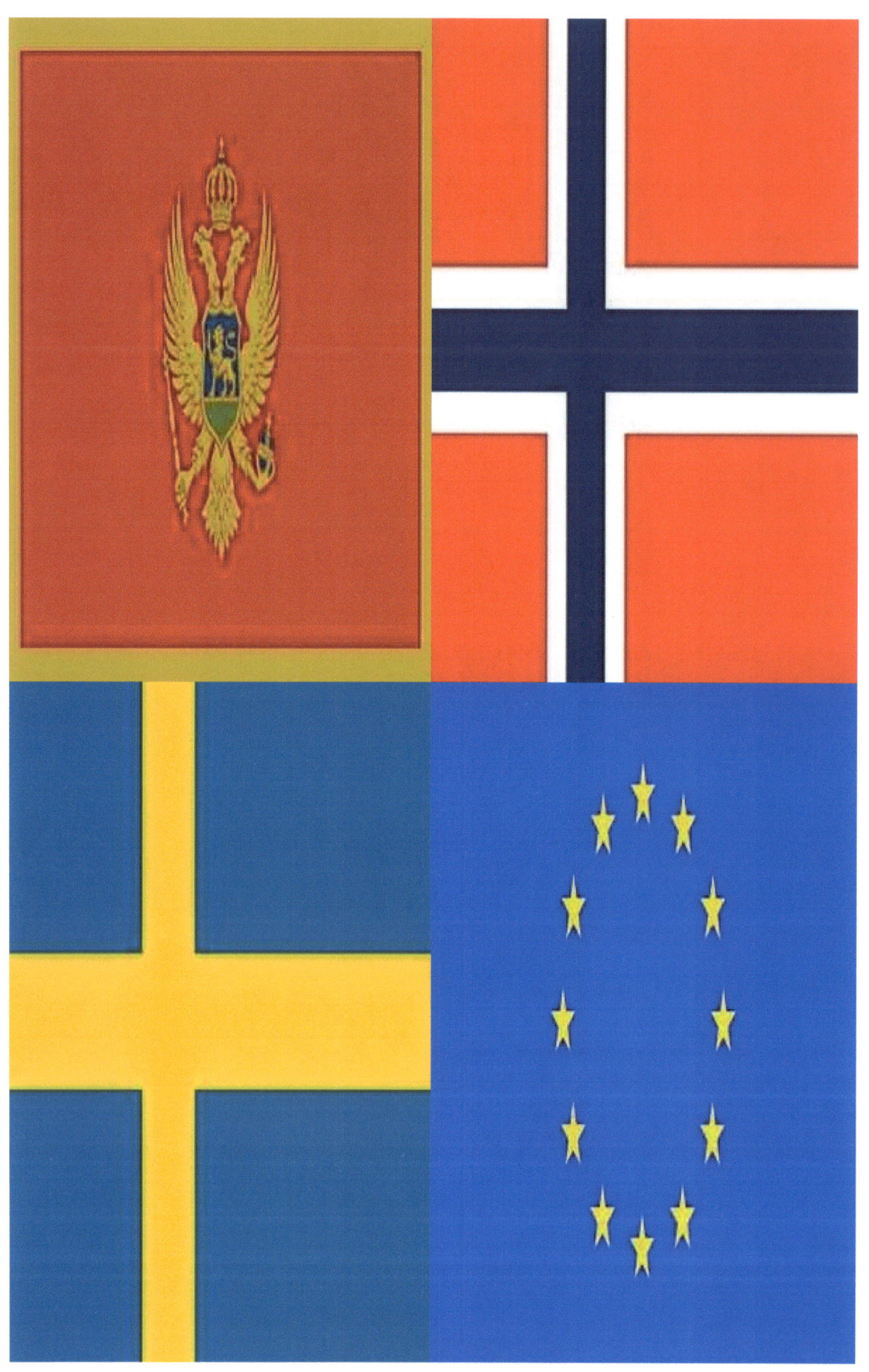

Arya Bàhram

Our Europe

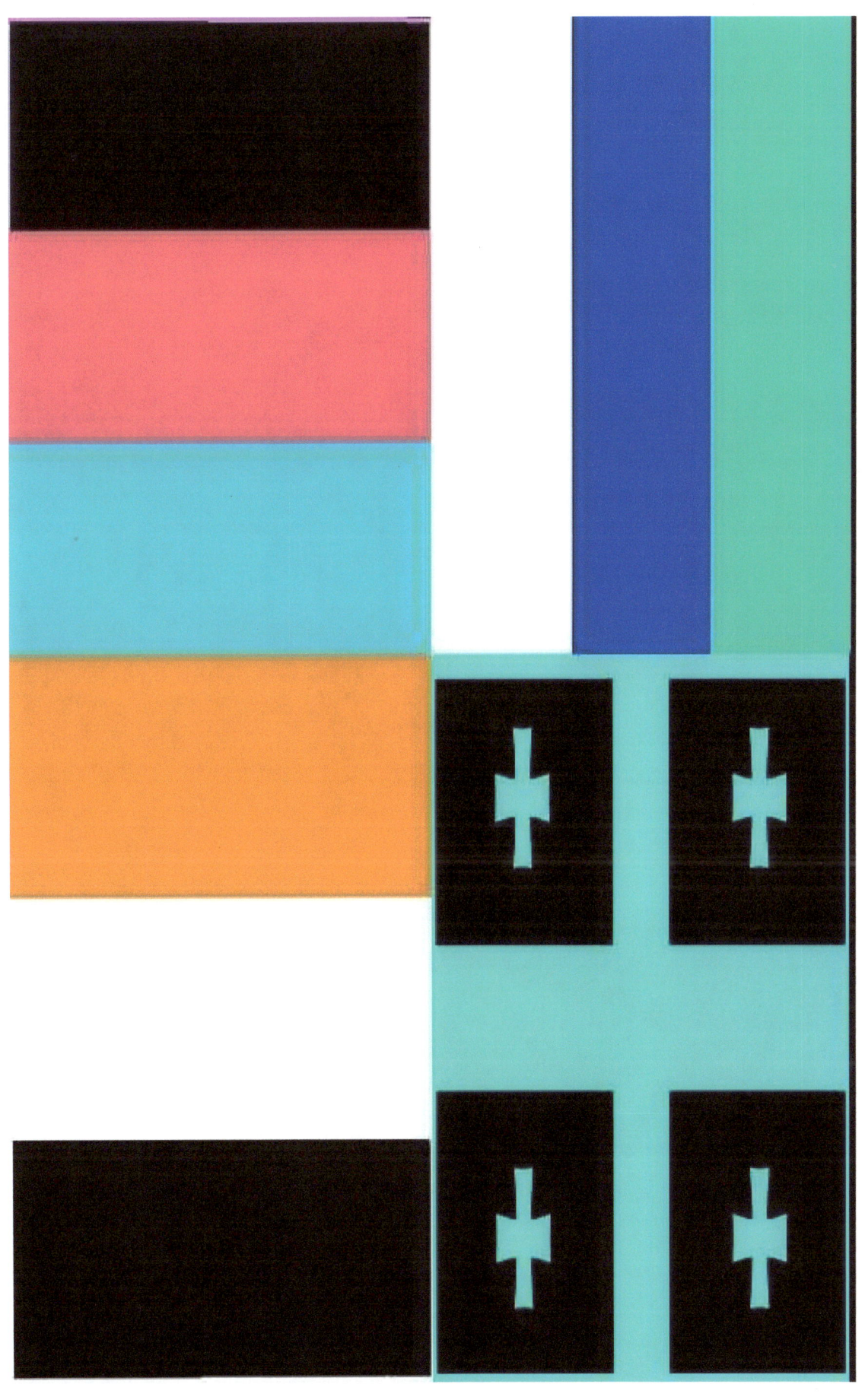

Arya Bàhram

Our Europe

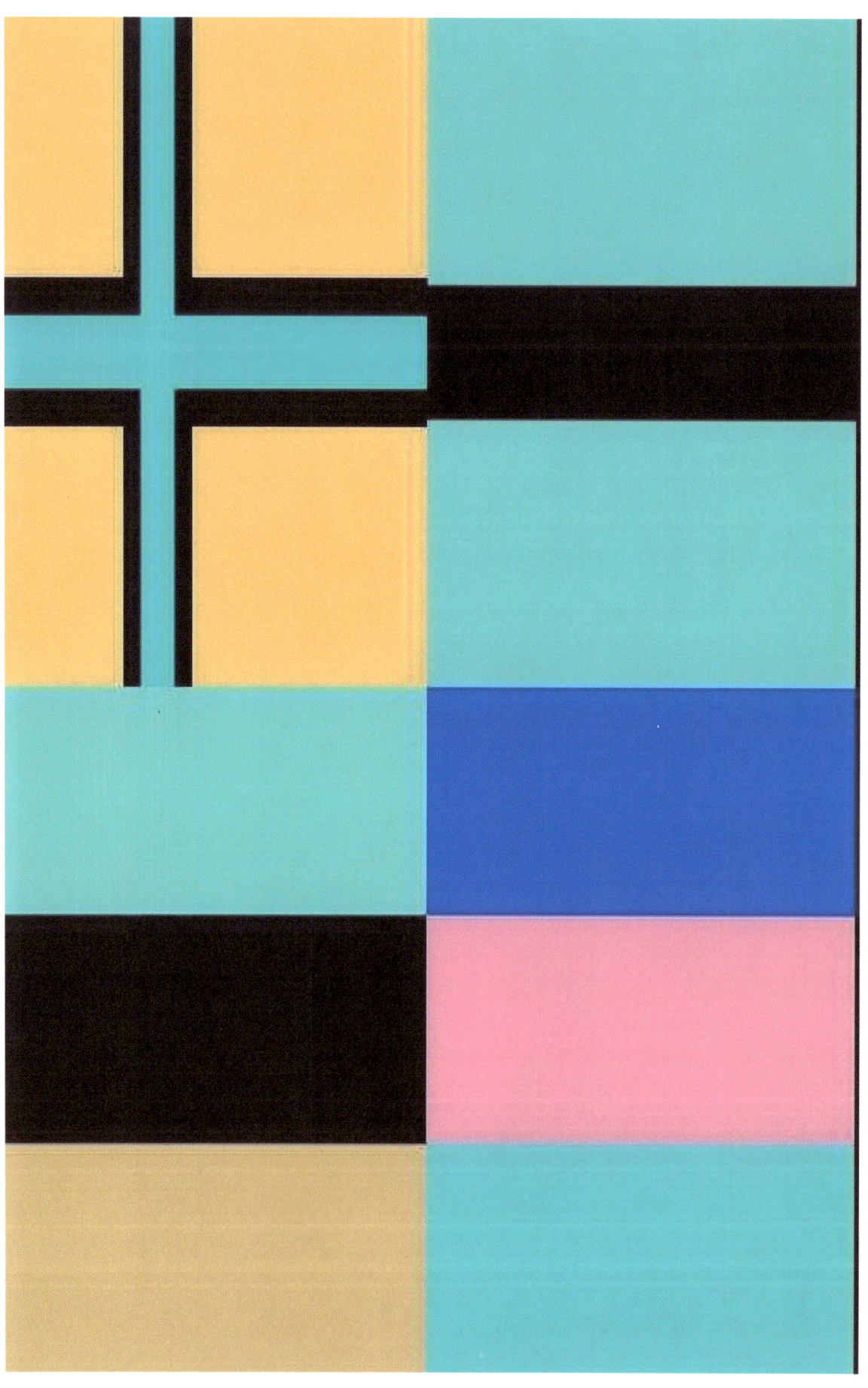

Arya Bàhram

Our Europe

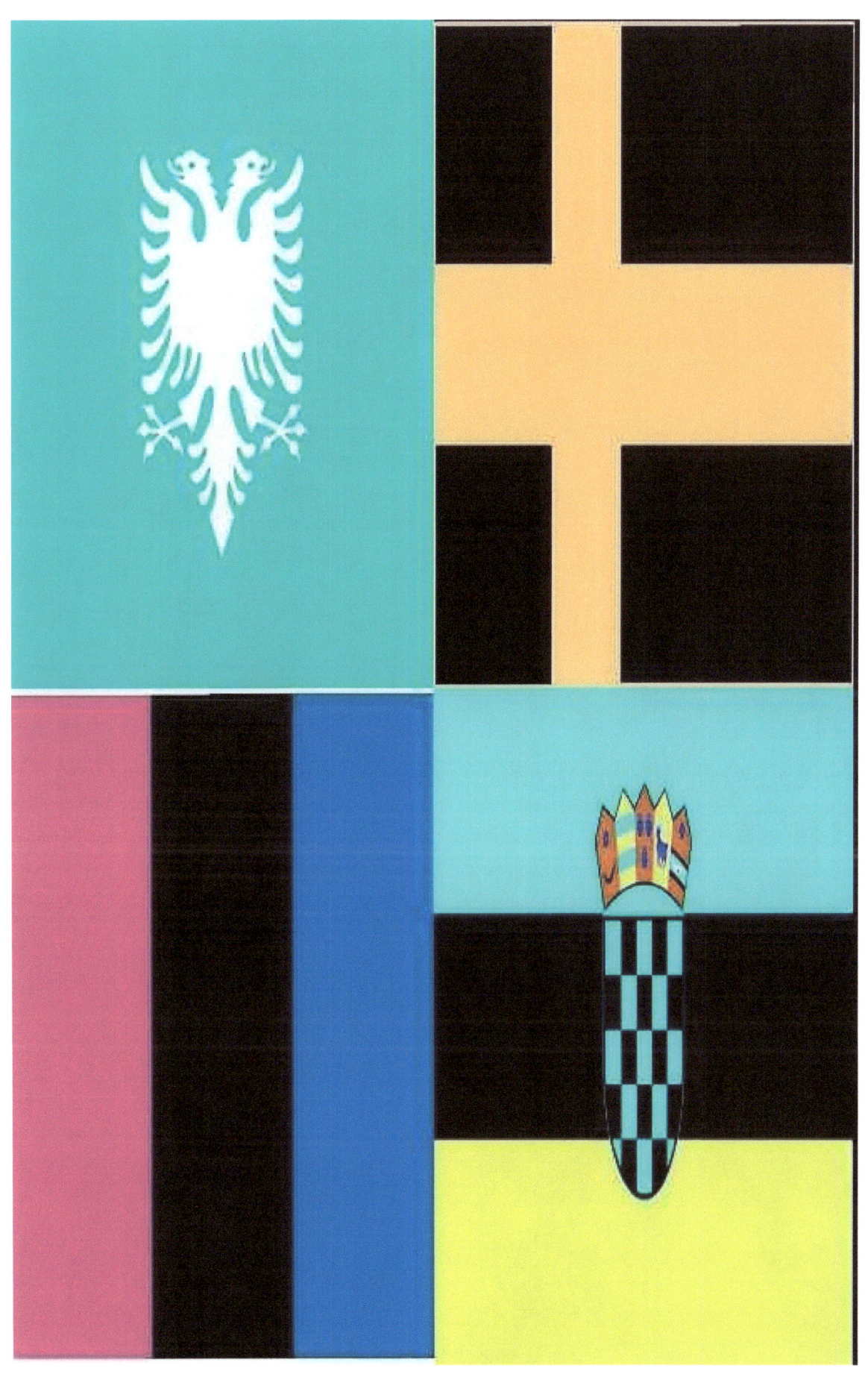

Arya Bàhram

Our Europe

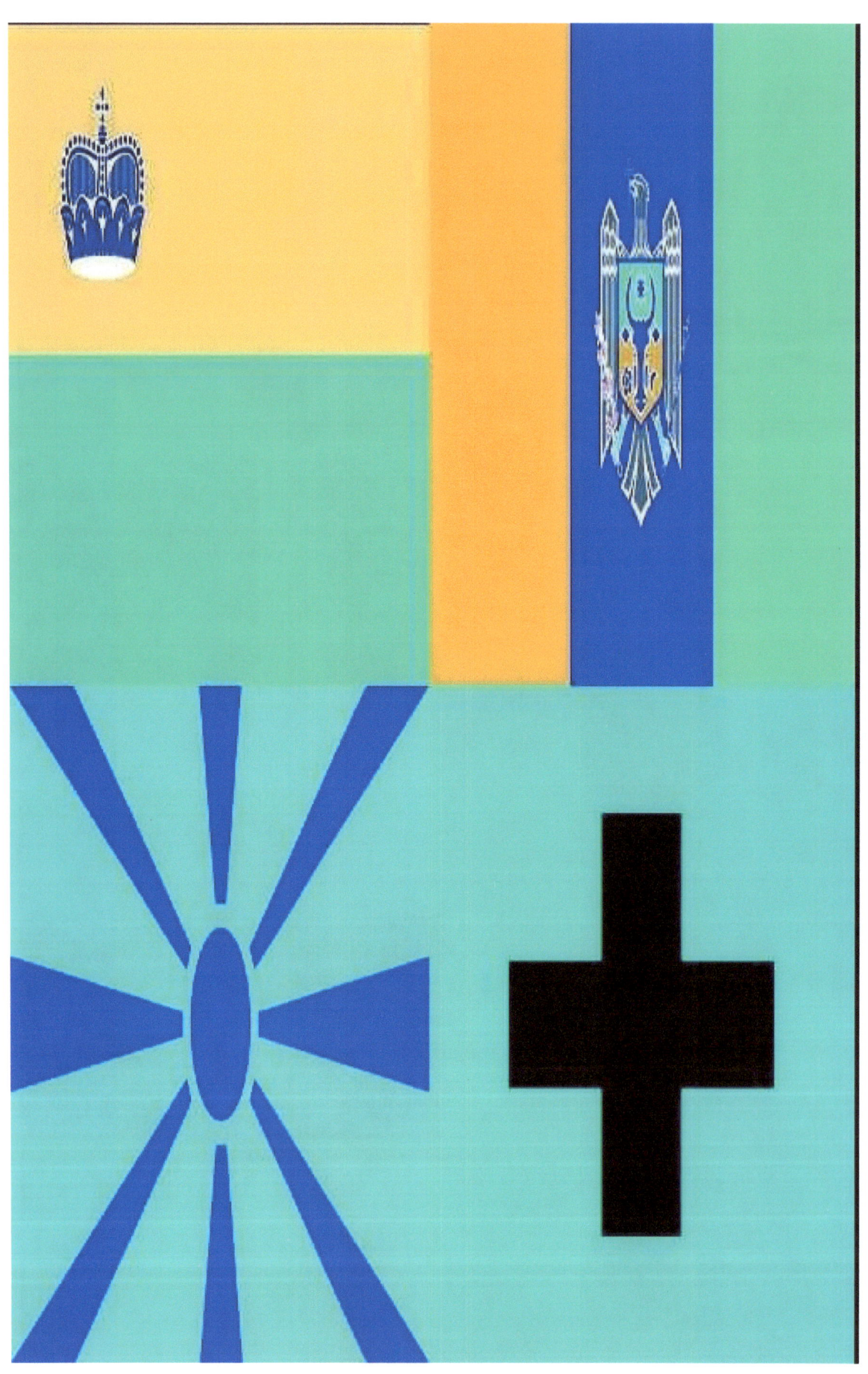

Arya Bàhram

Our Europe

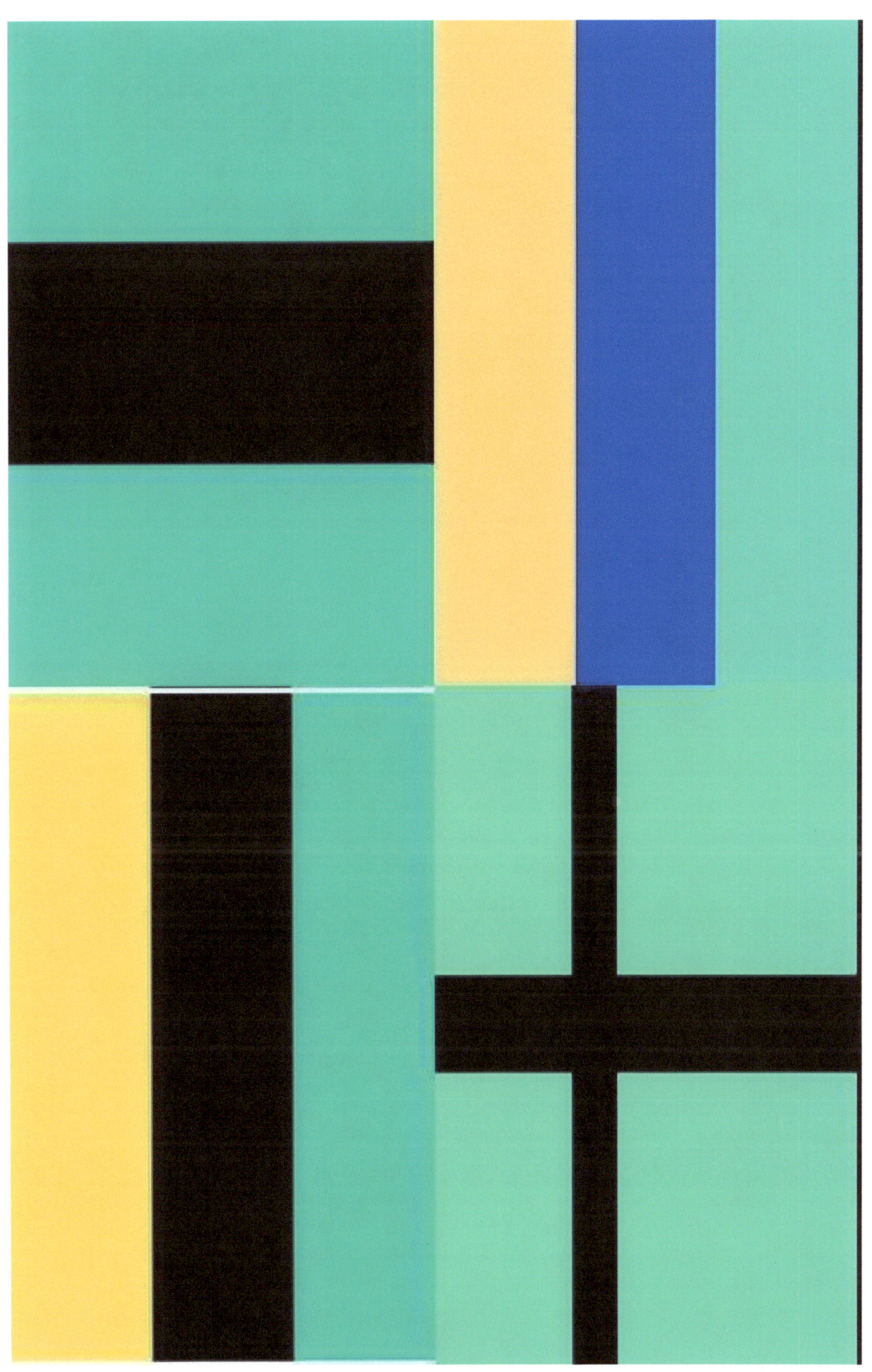

Arya Bàhram

Our Europe

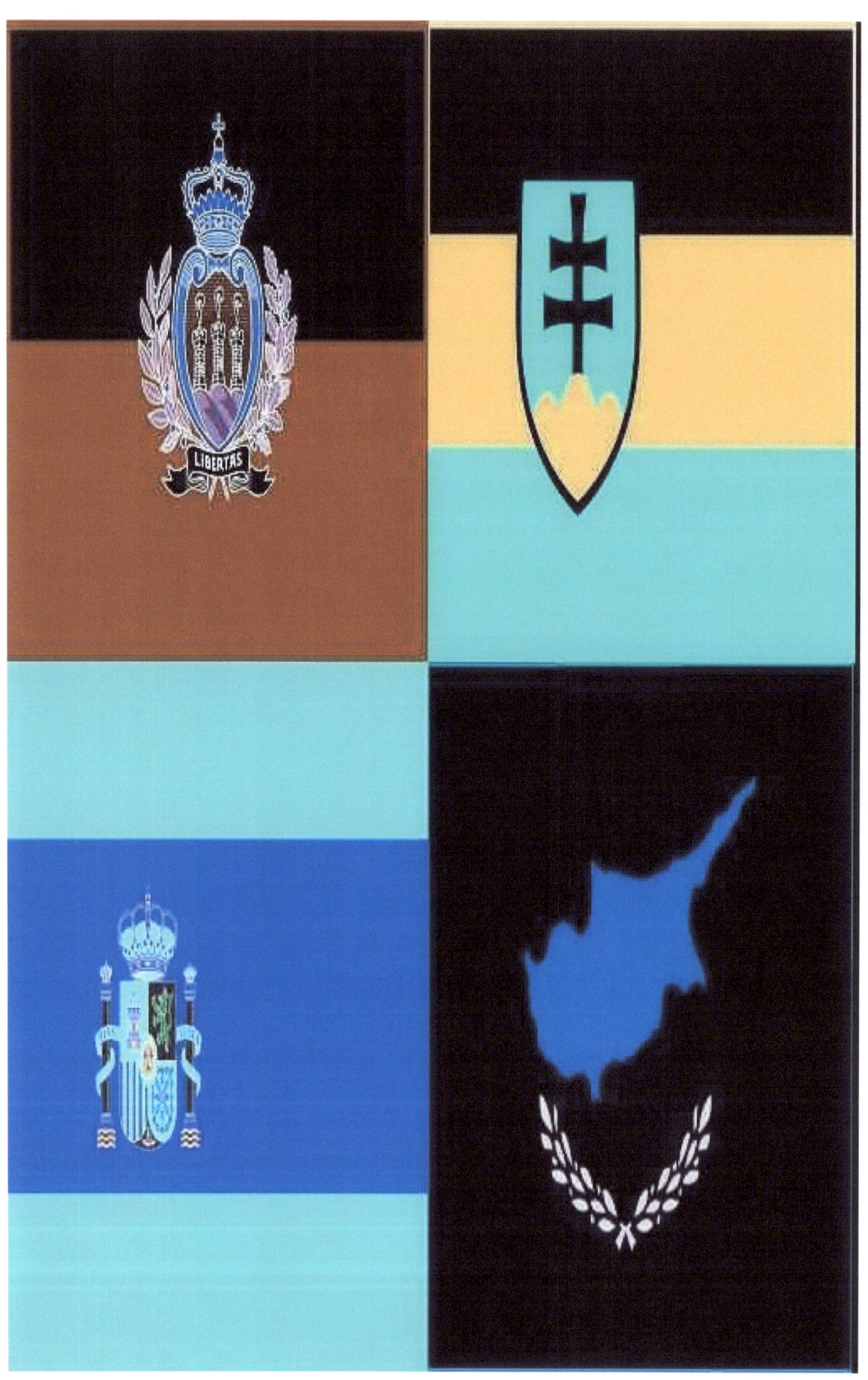

Arya Bàhram

Our Europe

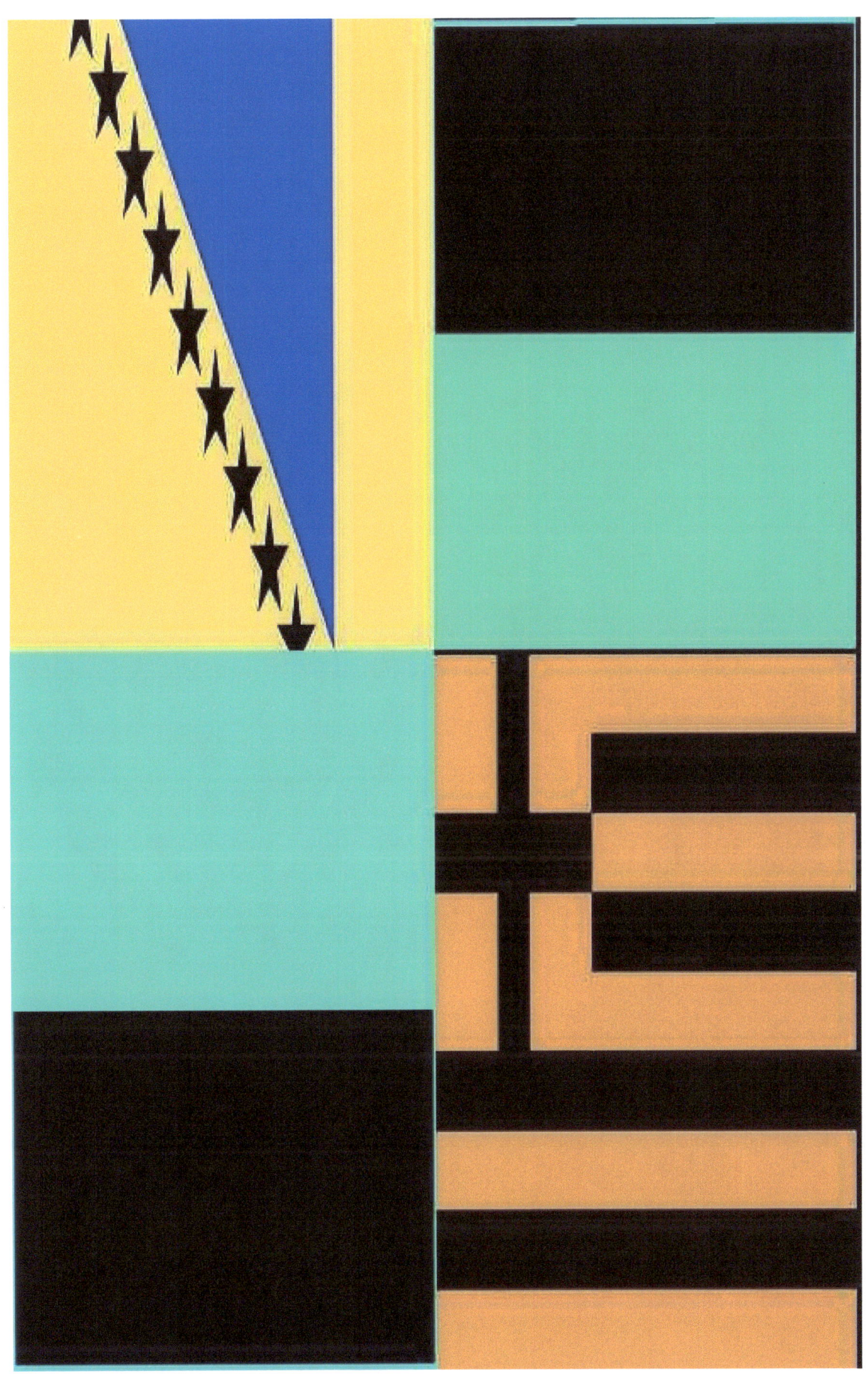

Arya Bàhram

Our Europe

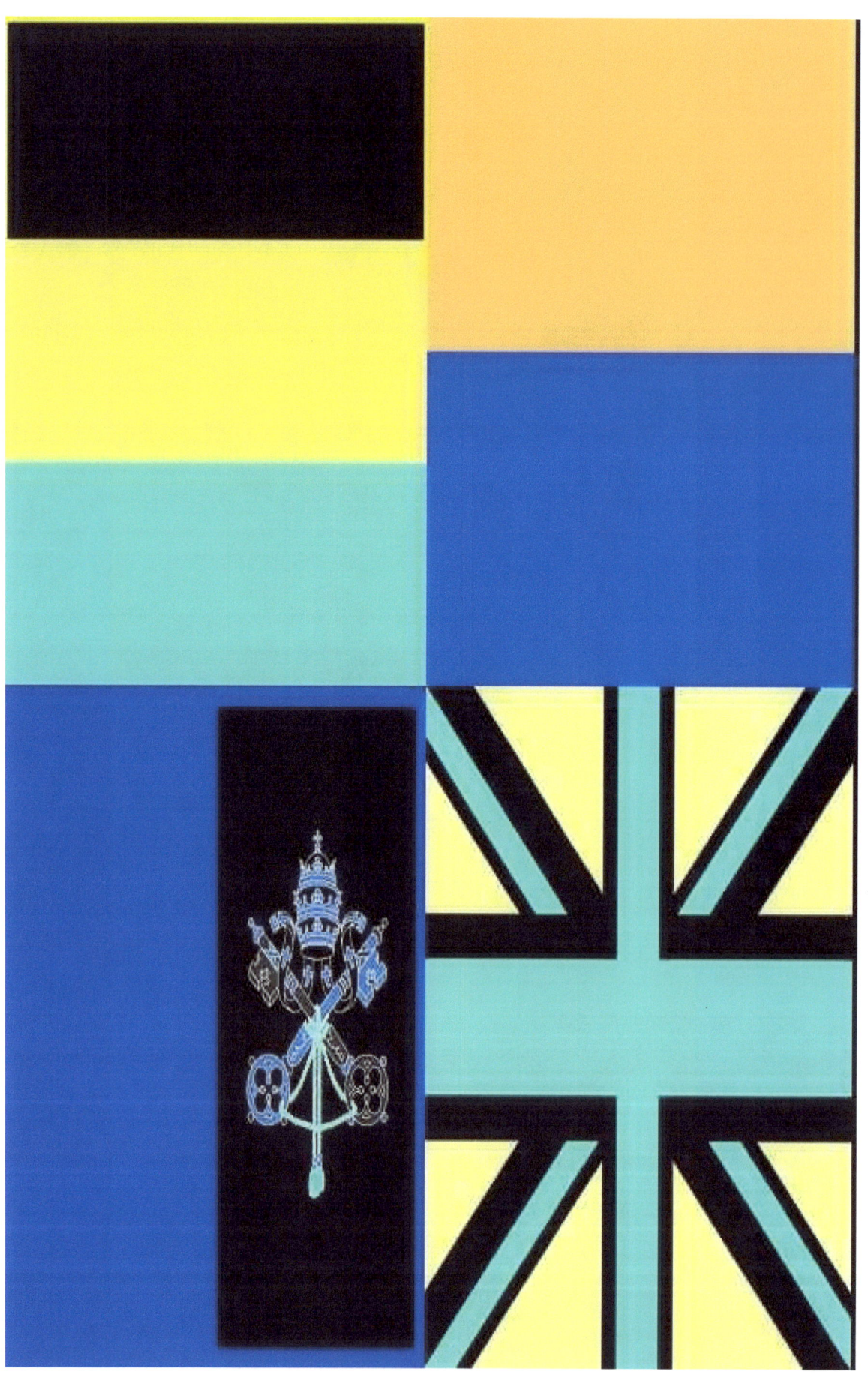

Arya Bàhram

Our Europe

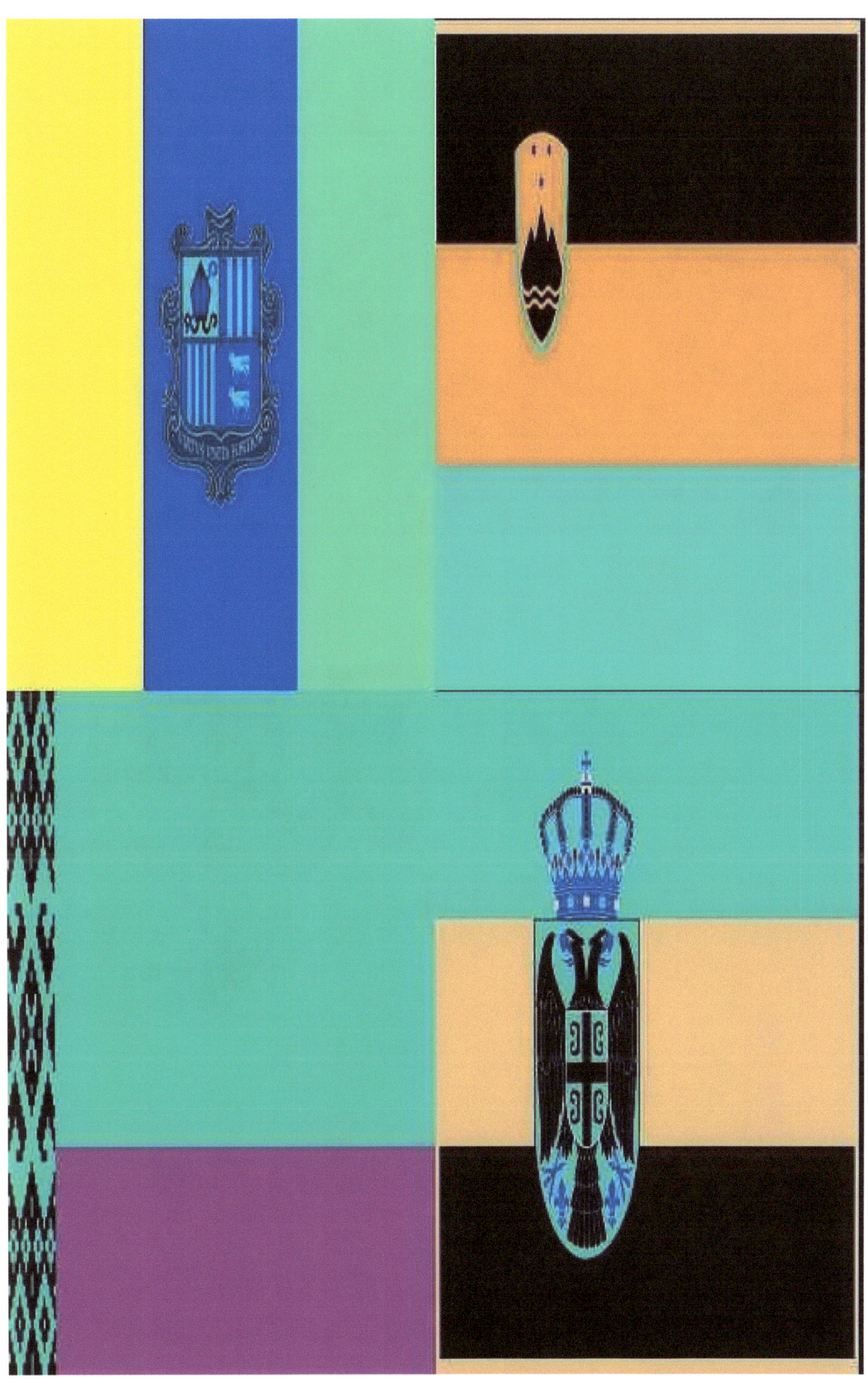

Arya Bàhram

Our Europe

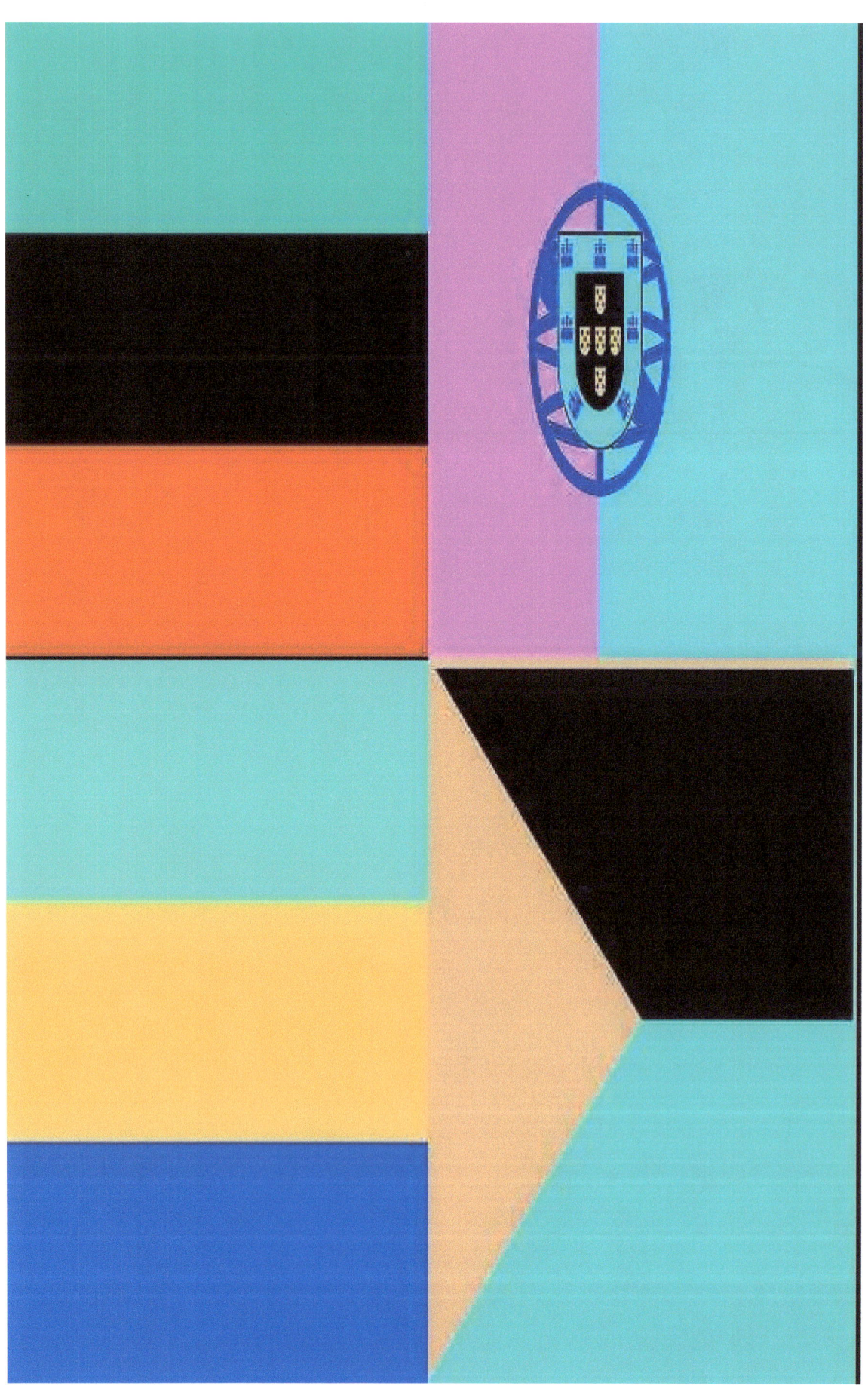

Arya Bàhram

Our Europe

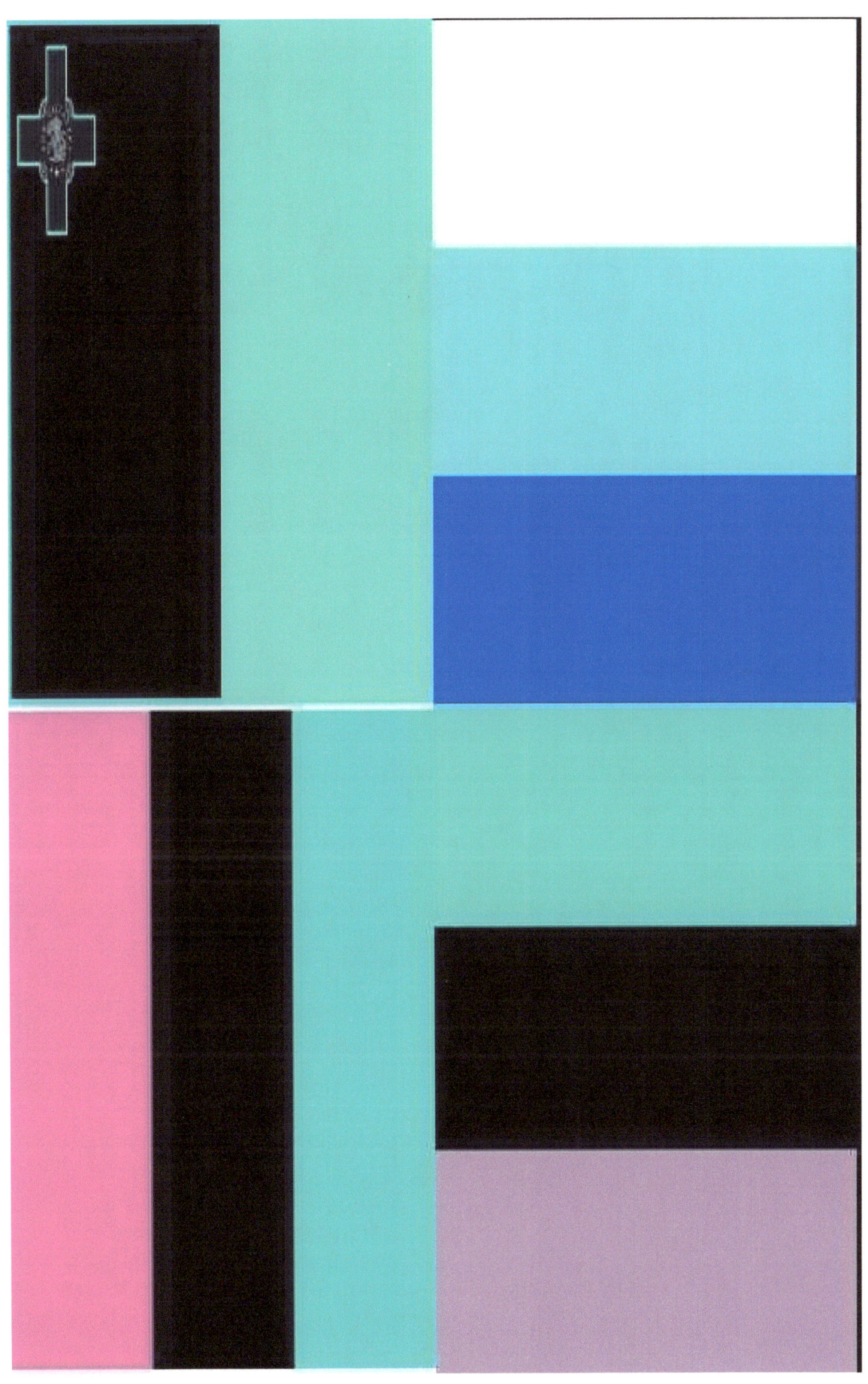

Arya Bàhram

Our Europe

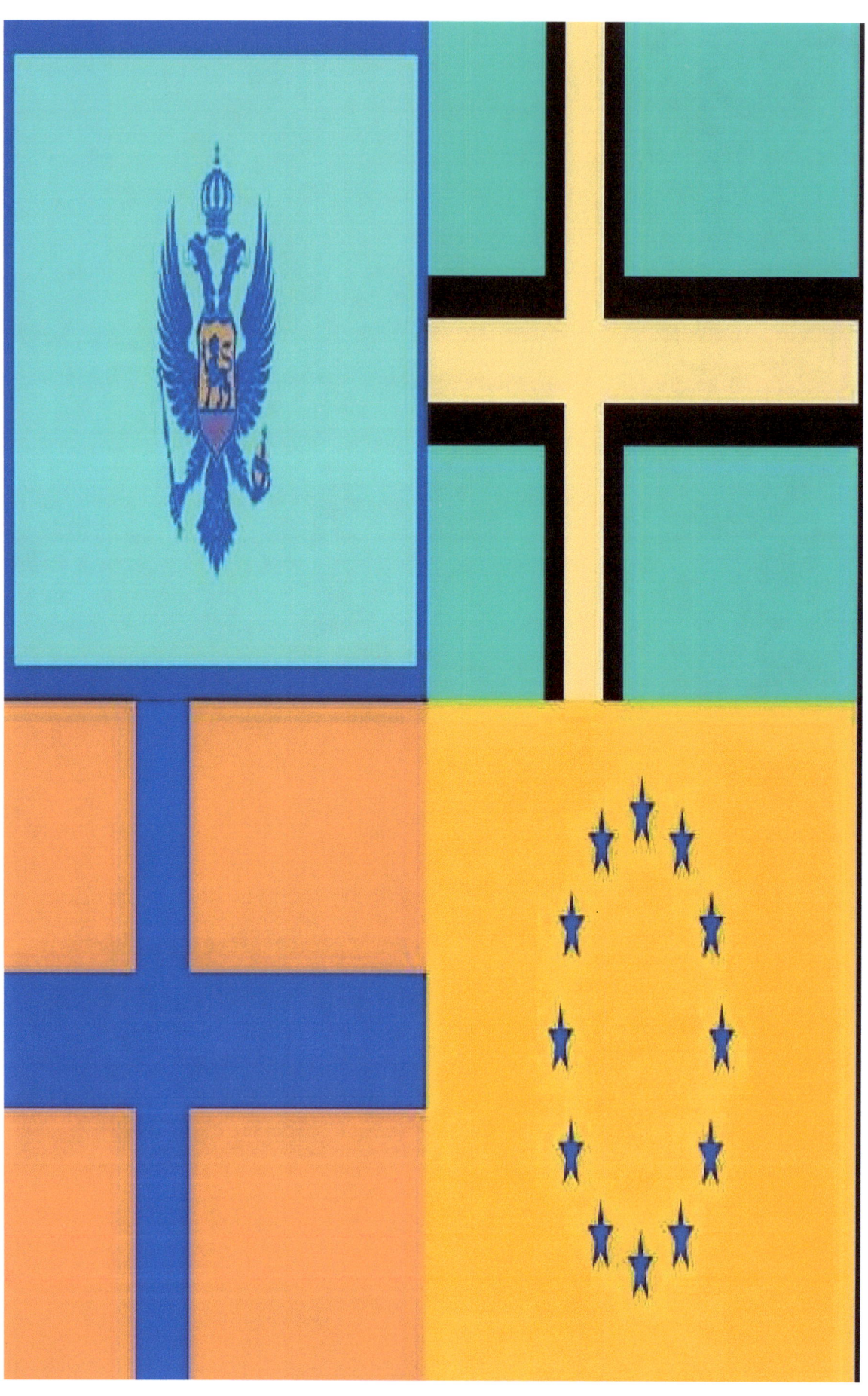

Arya Bàhram

Our Europe

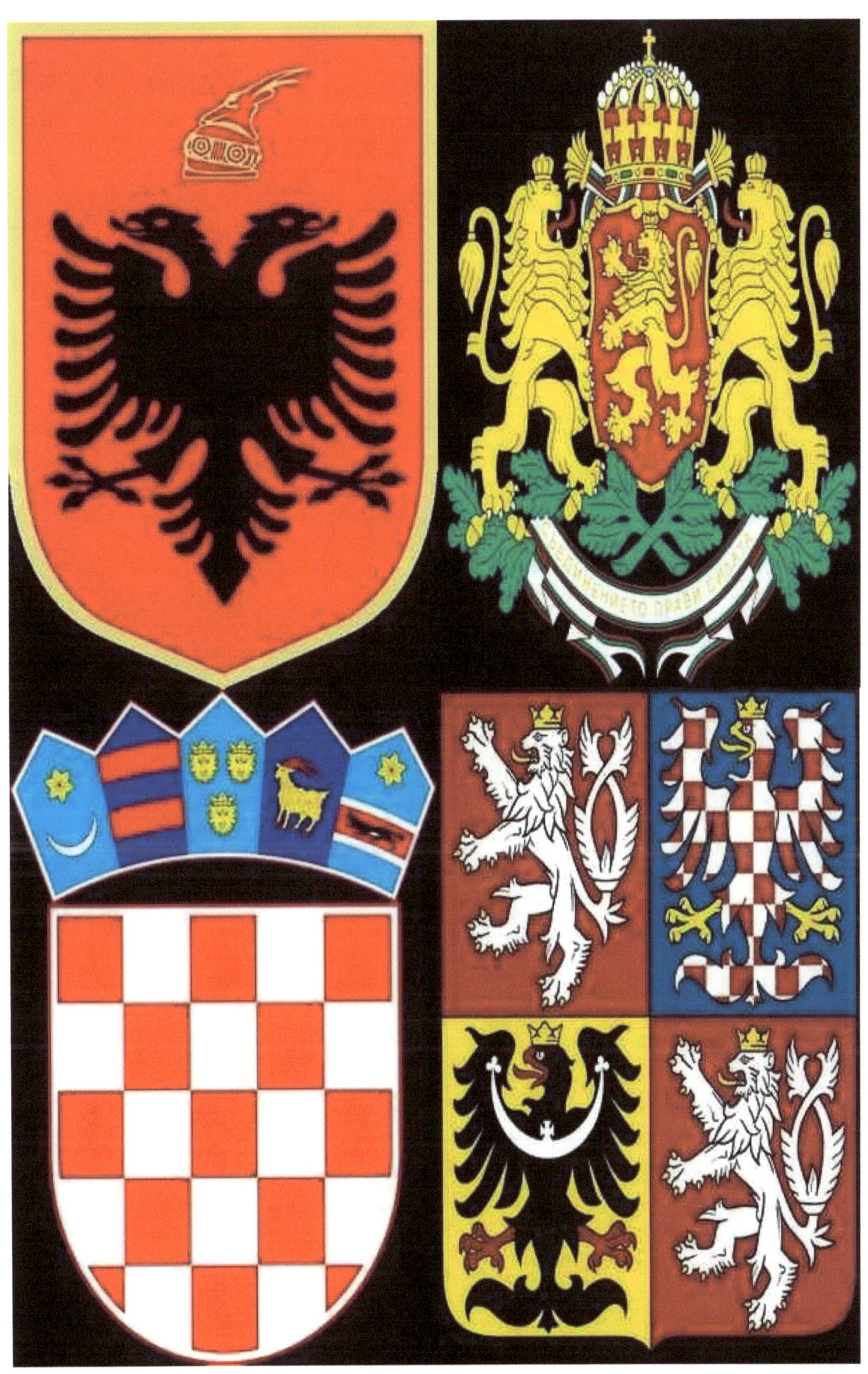

Arya Bàhram

Our Europe

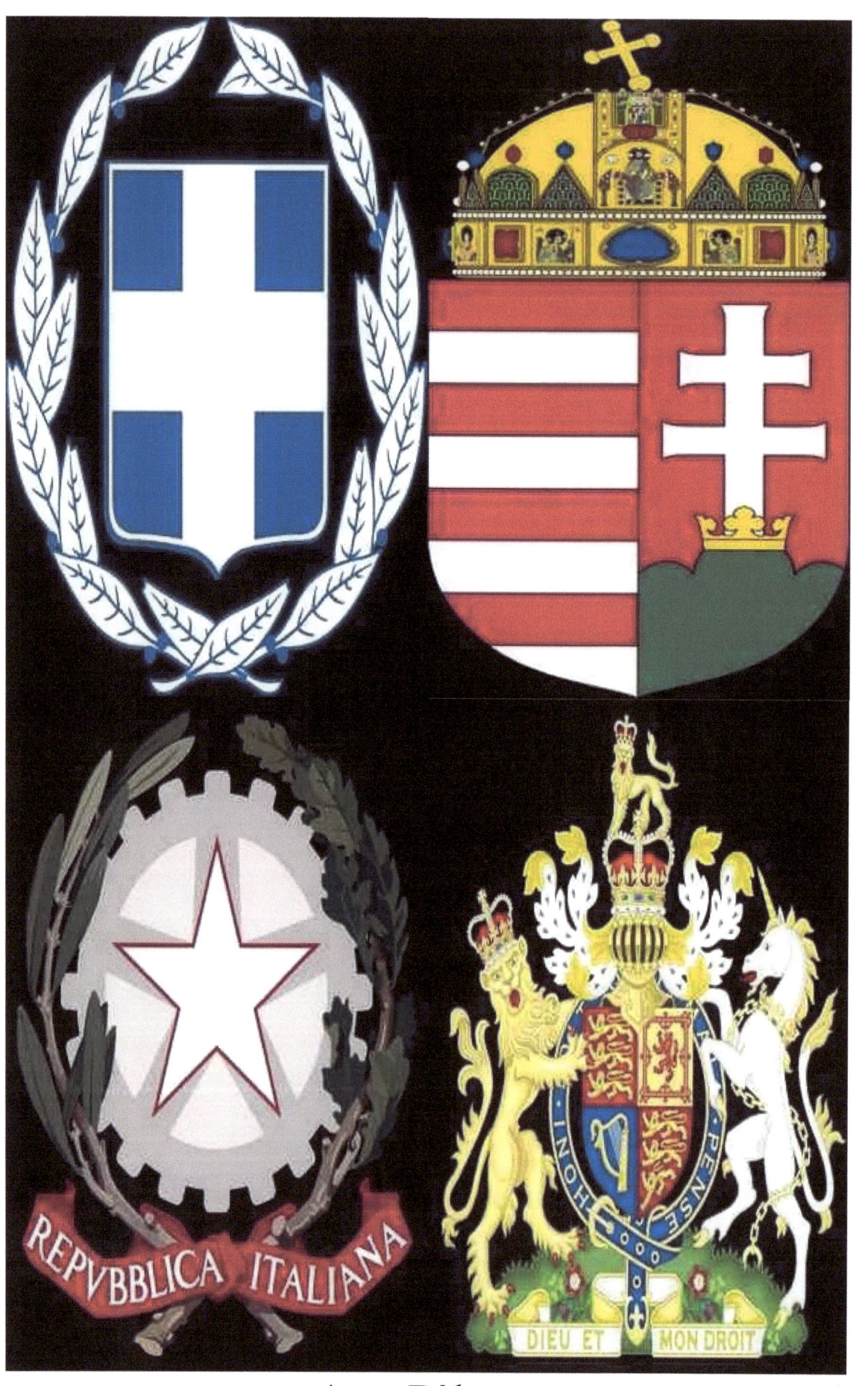

Arya Bàhram

Our Europe

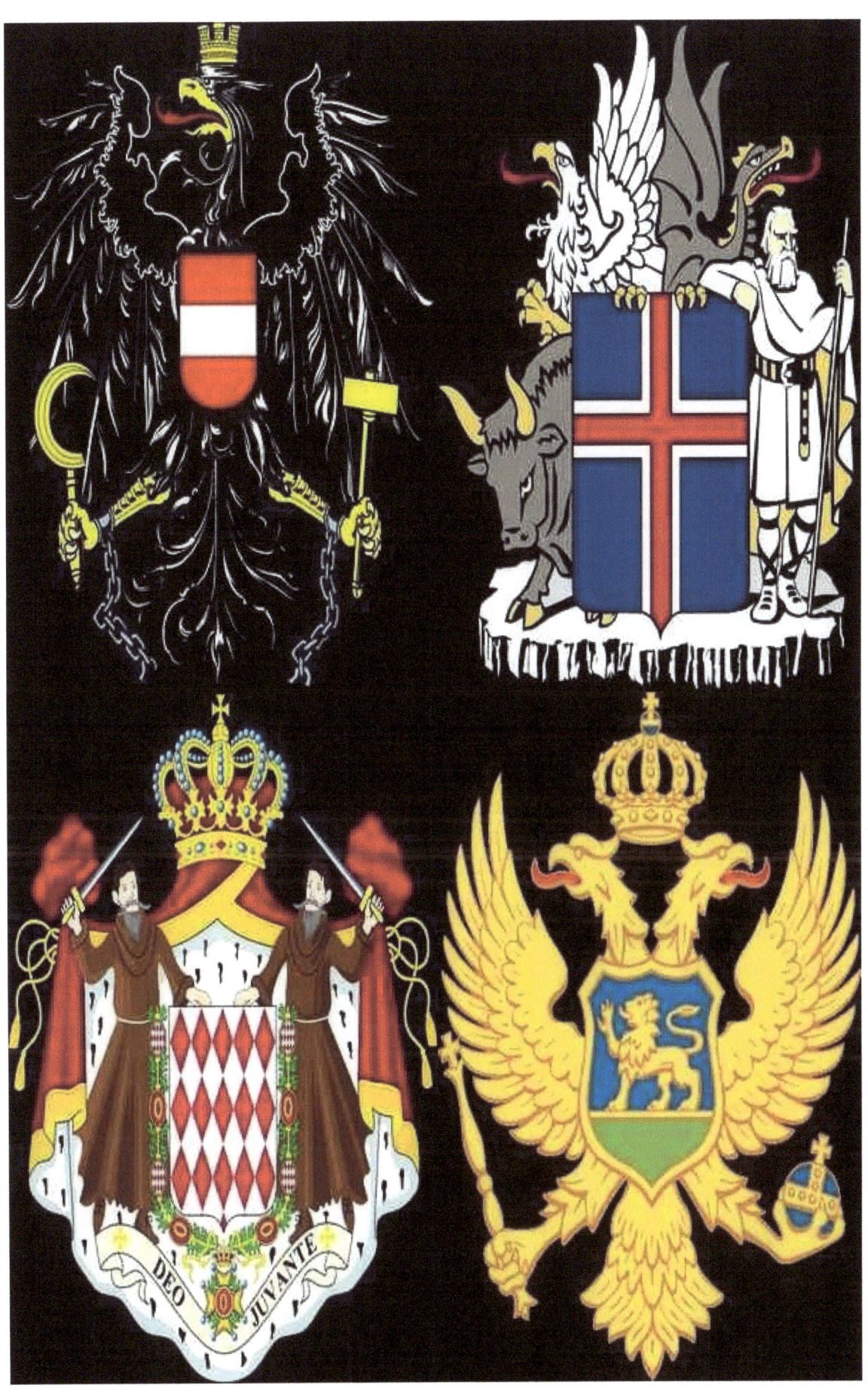

Arya Bàhram

Our Europe

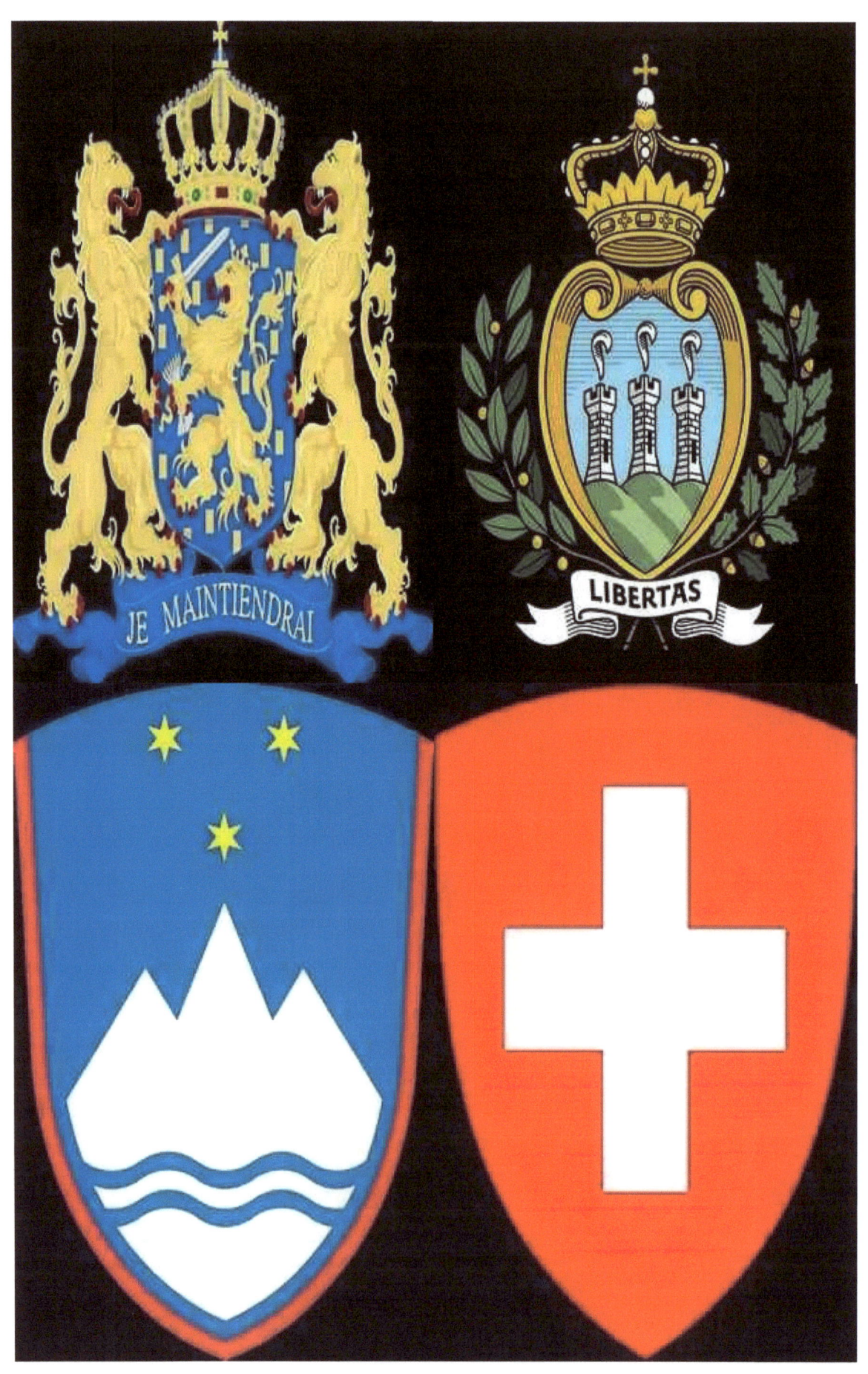

Arya Bàhram

Our Europe

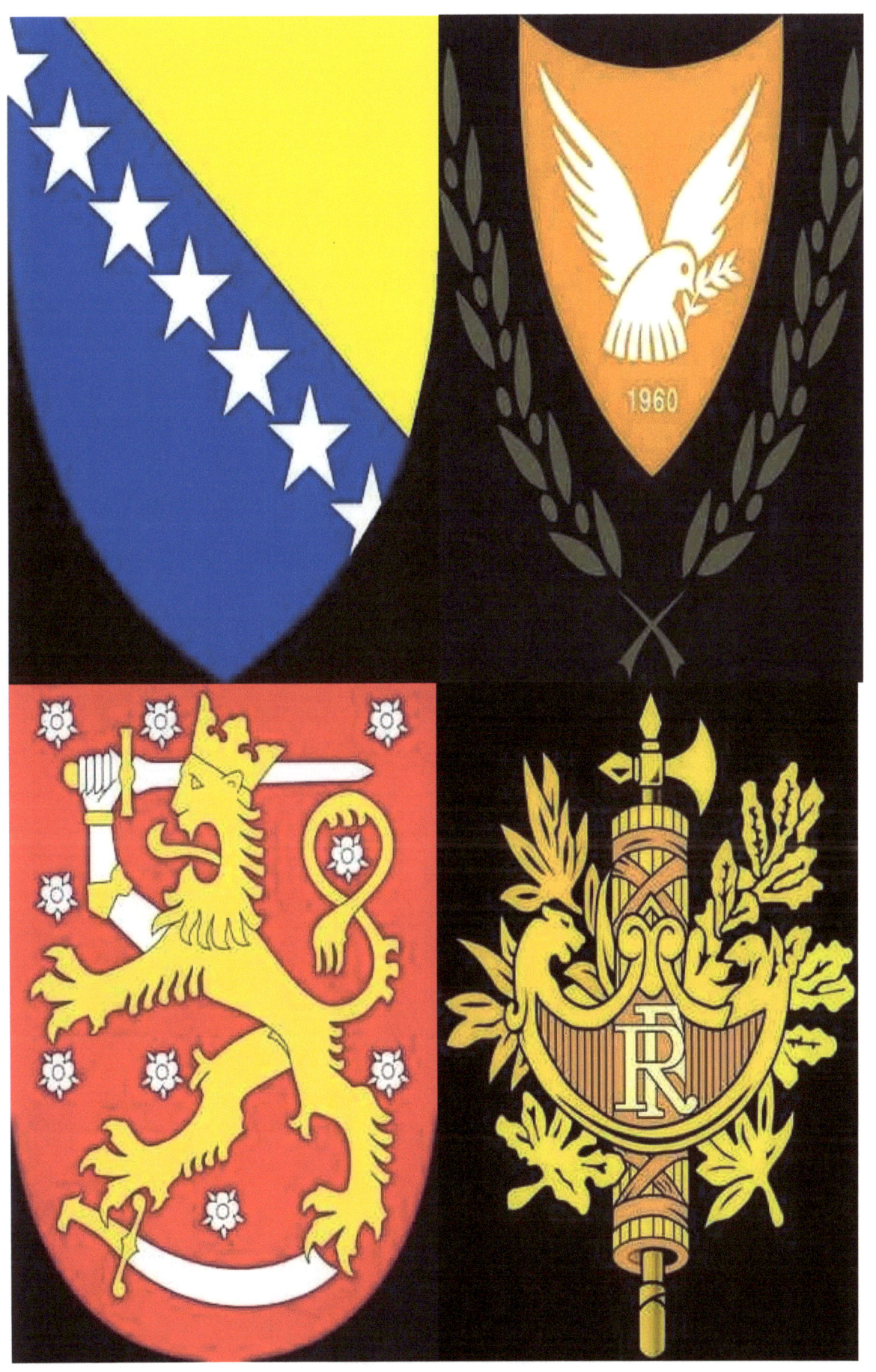

Arya Bàhram

Our Europe

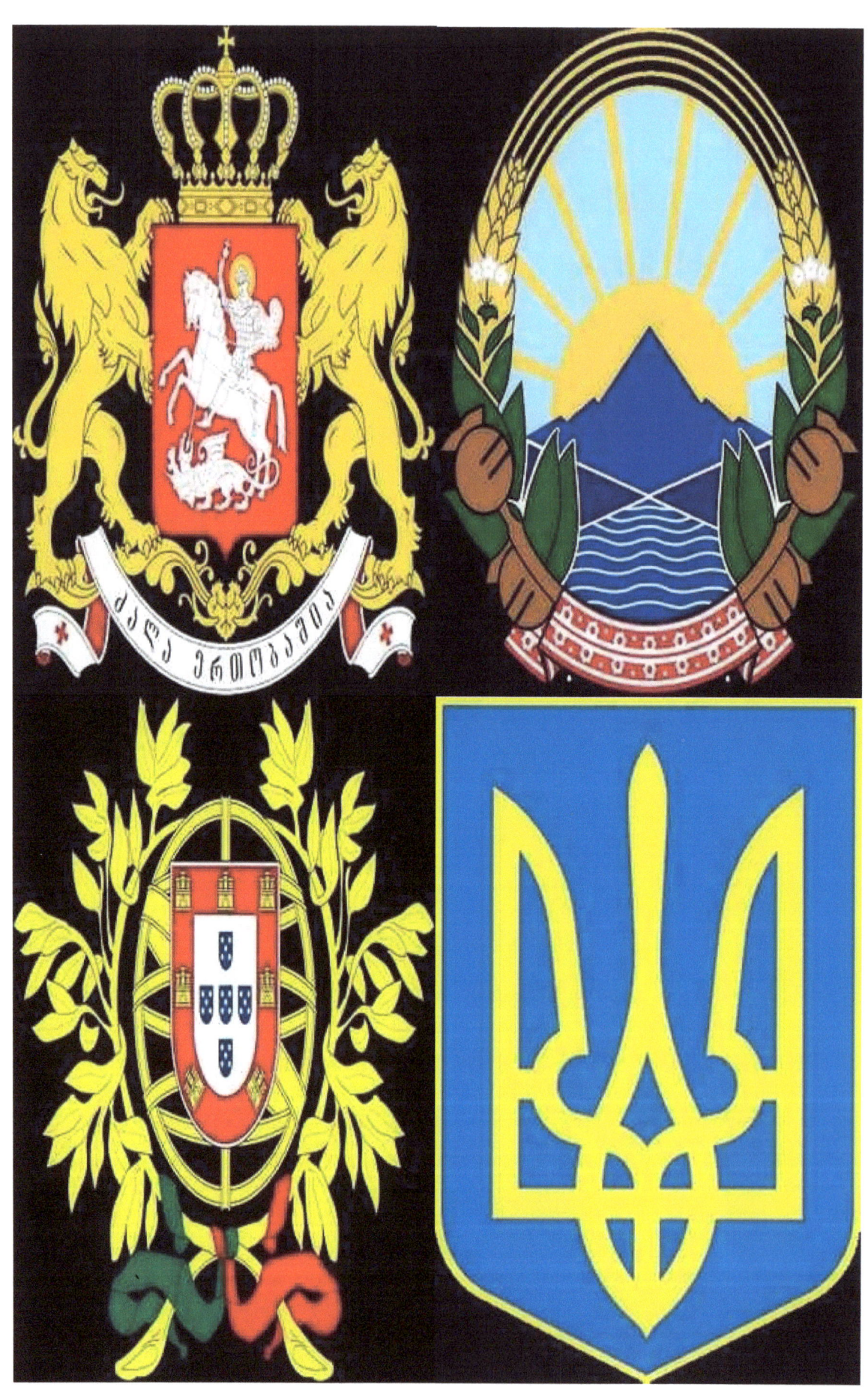

Arya Bàhram

Our Europe

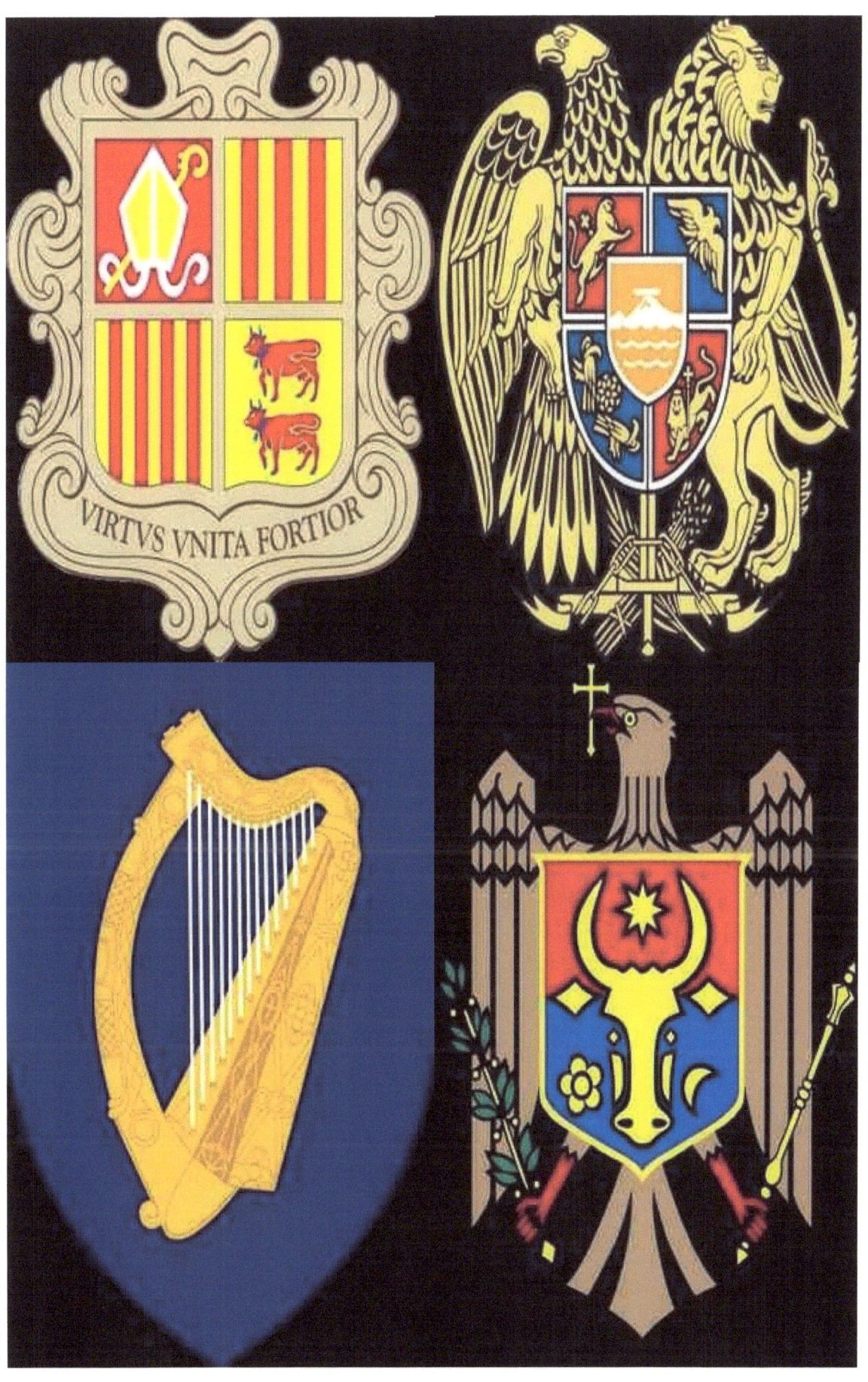

VIRTVS VNITA FORTIOR

Arya Bàhram

Our Europe

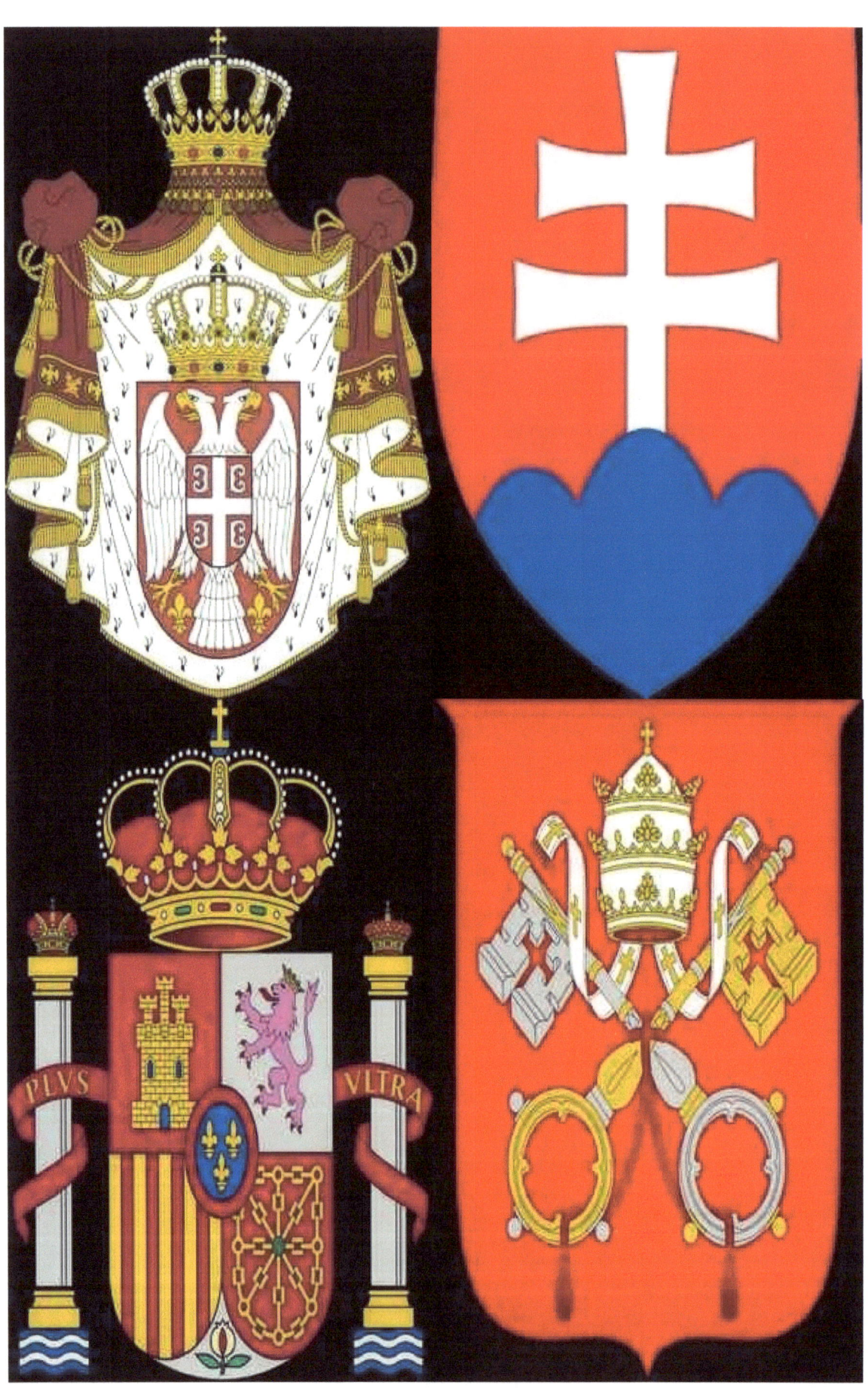

Arya Bàhram

Our Europe

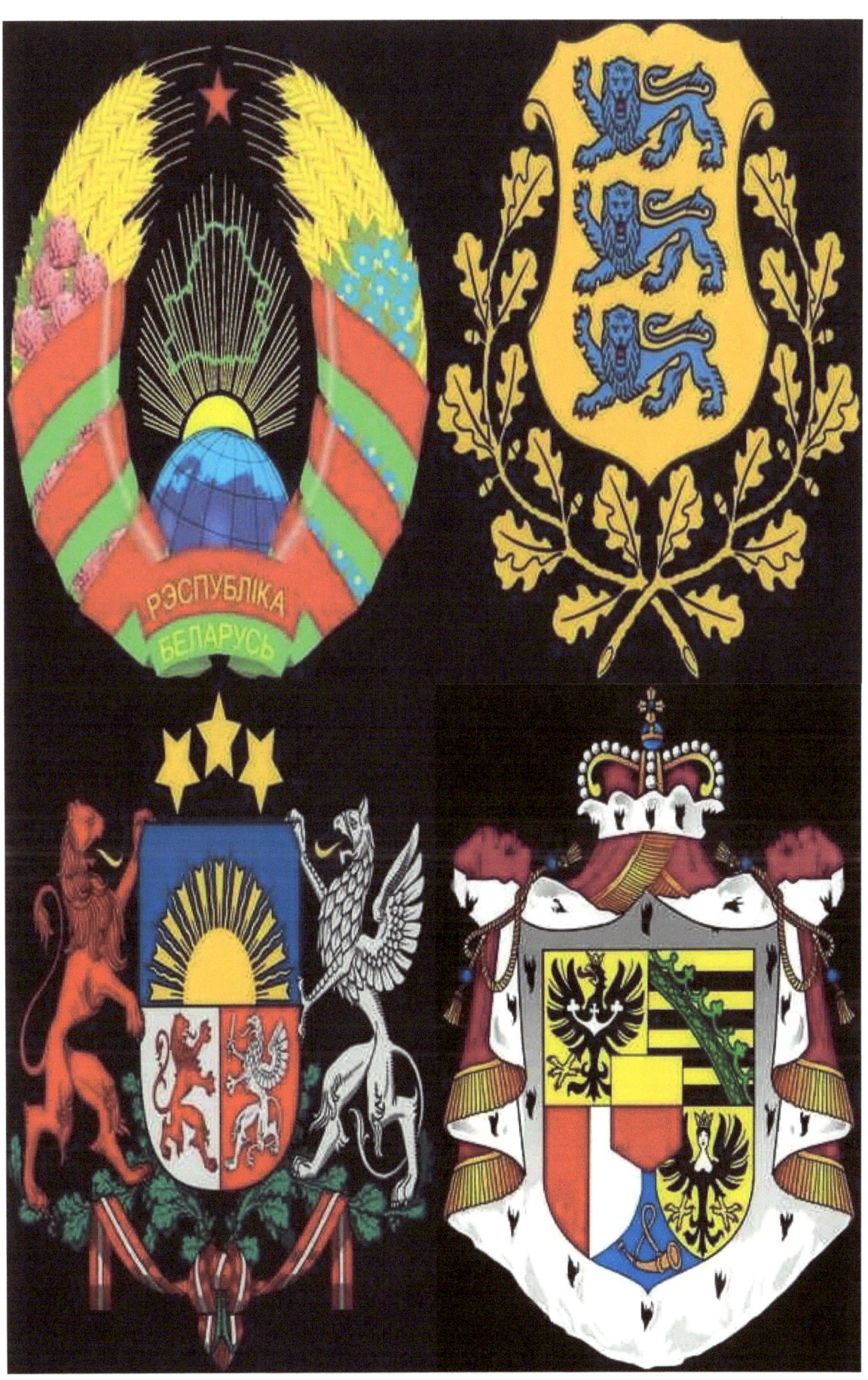

Arya Bàhram

Our Europe

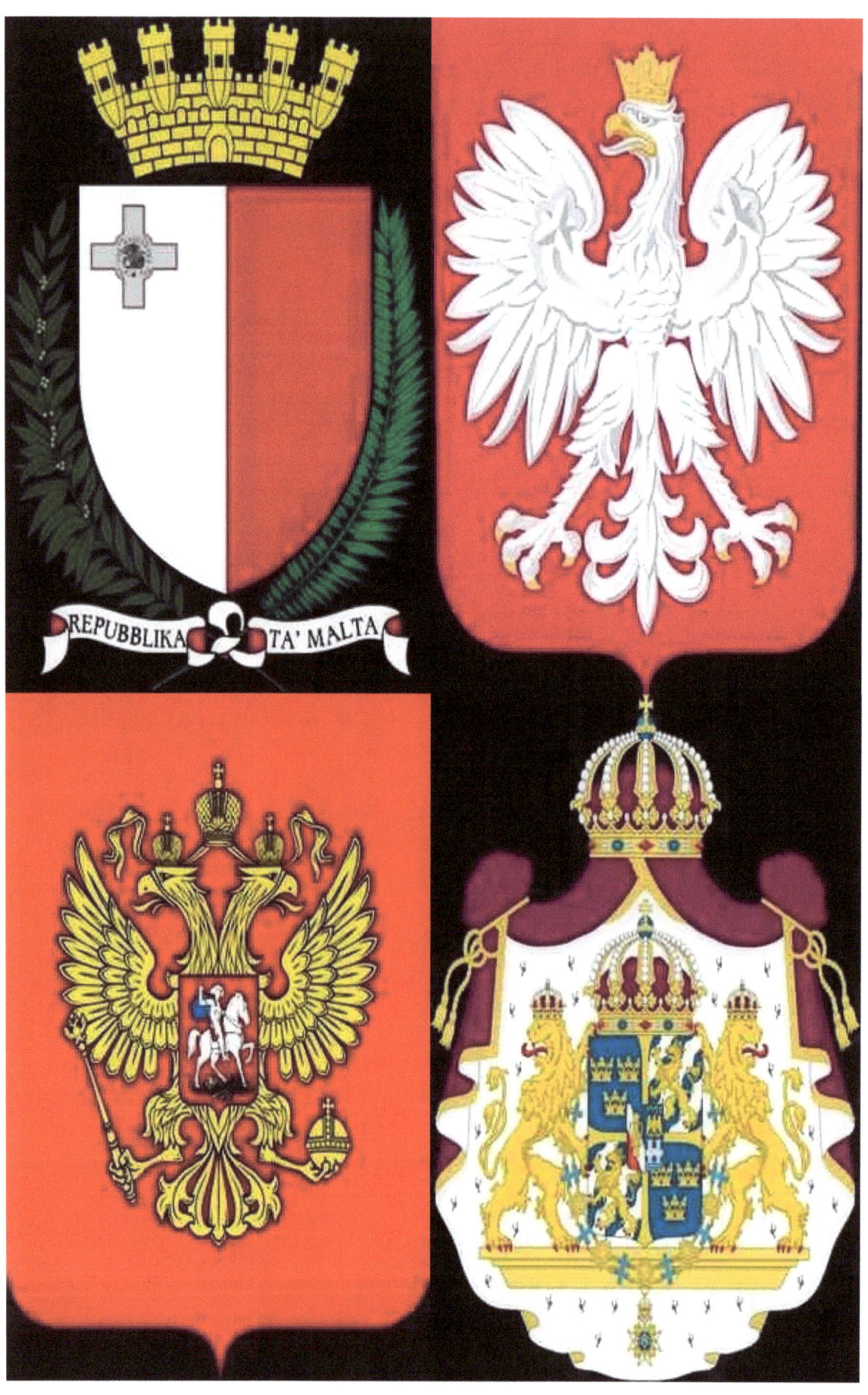

Arya Bàhram

Our Europe

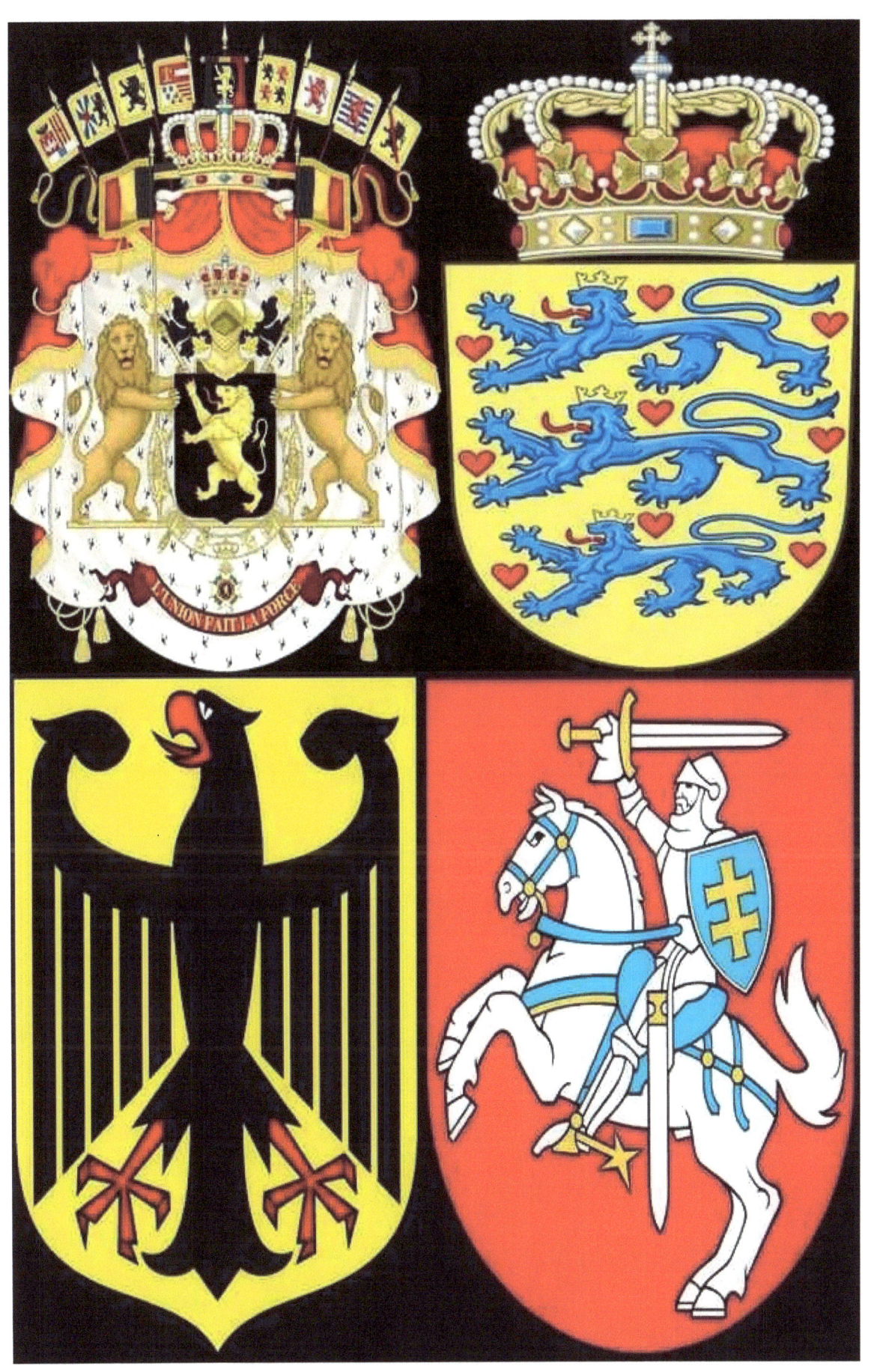

Arya Bàhram

Our Europe

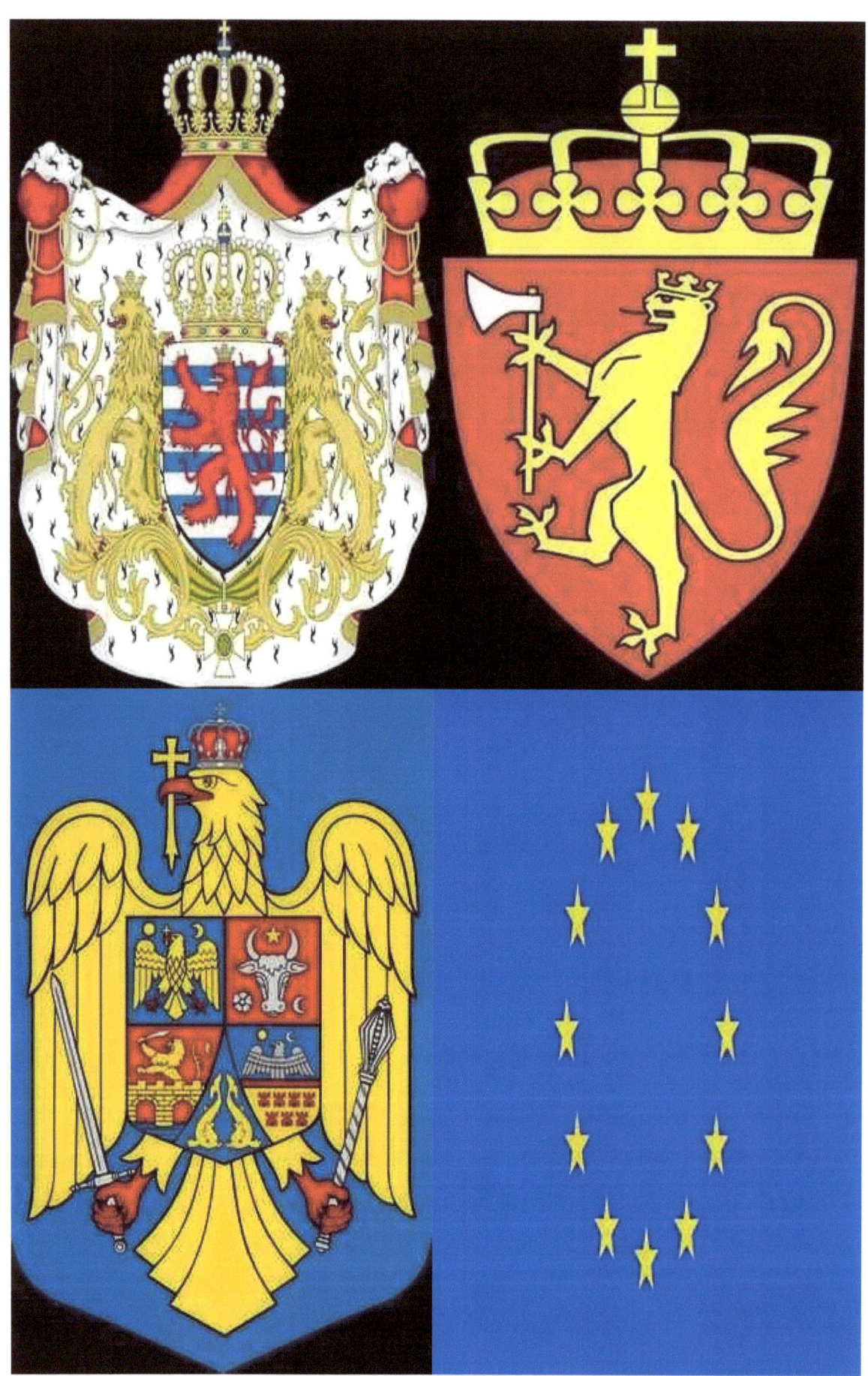

Arya Bàhram

Our Europe

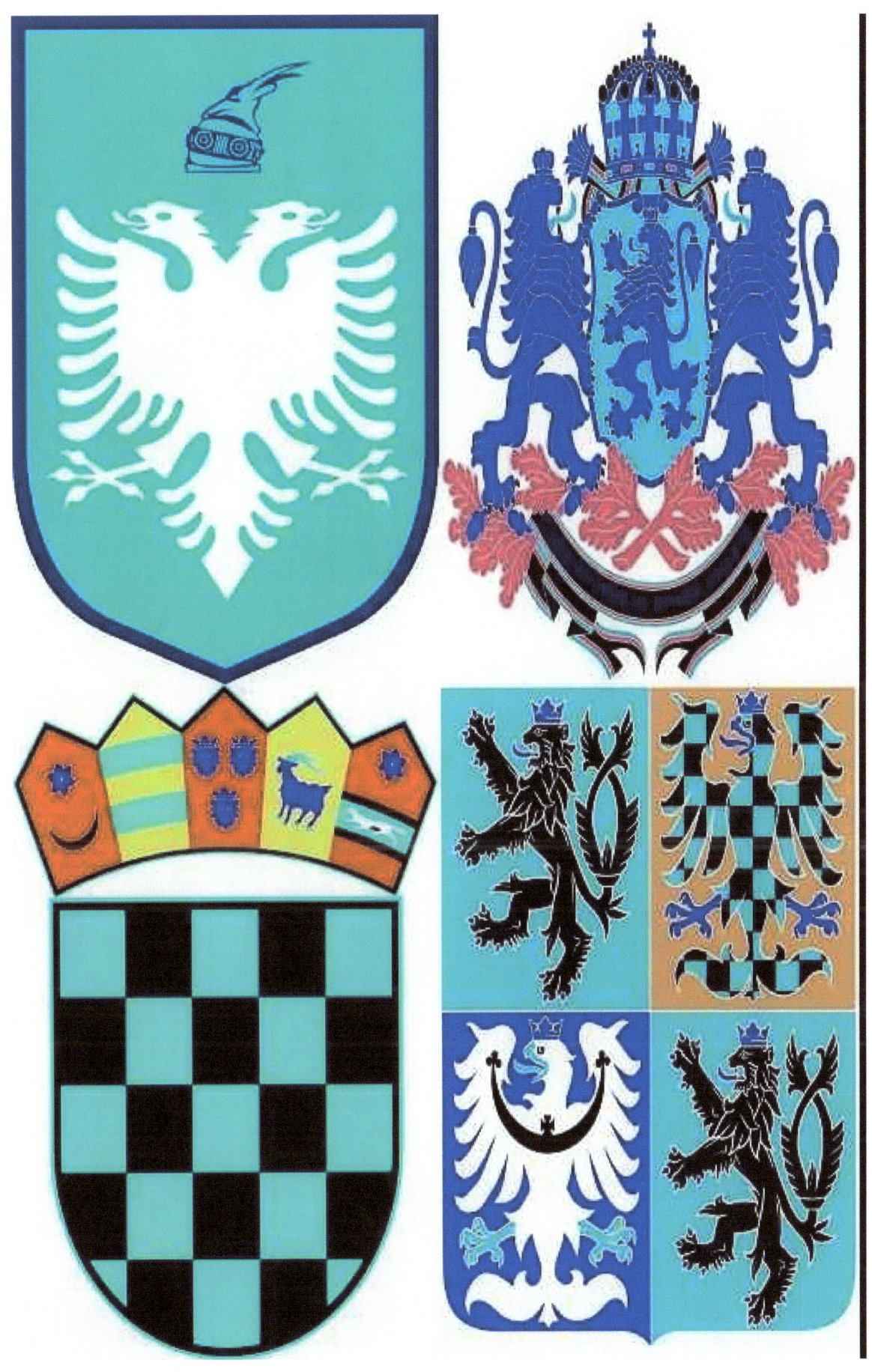

Arya Bàhram

Our Europe

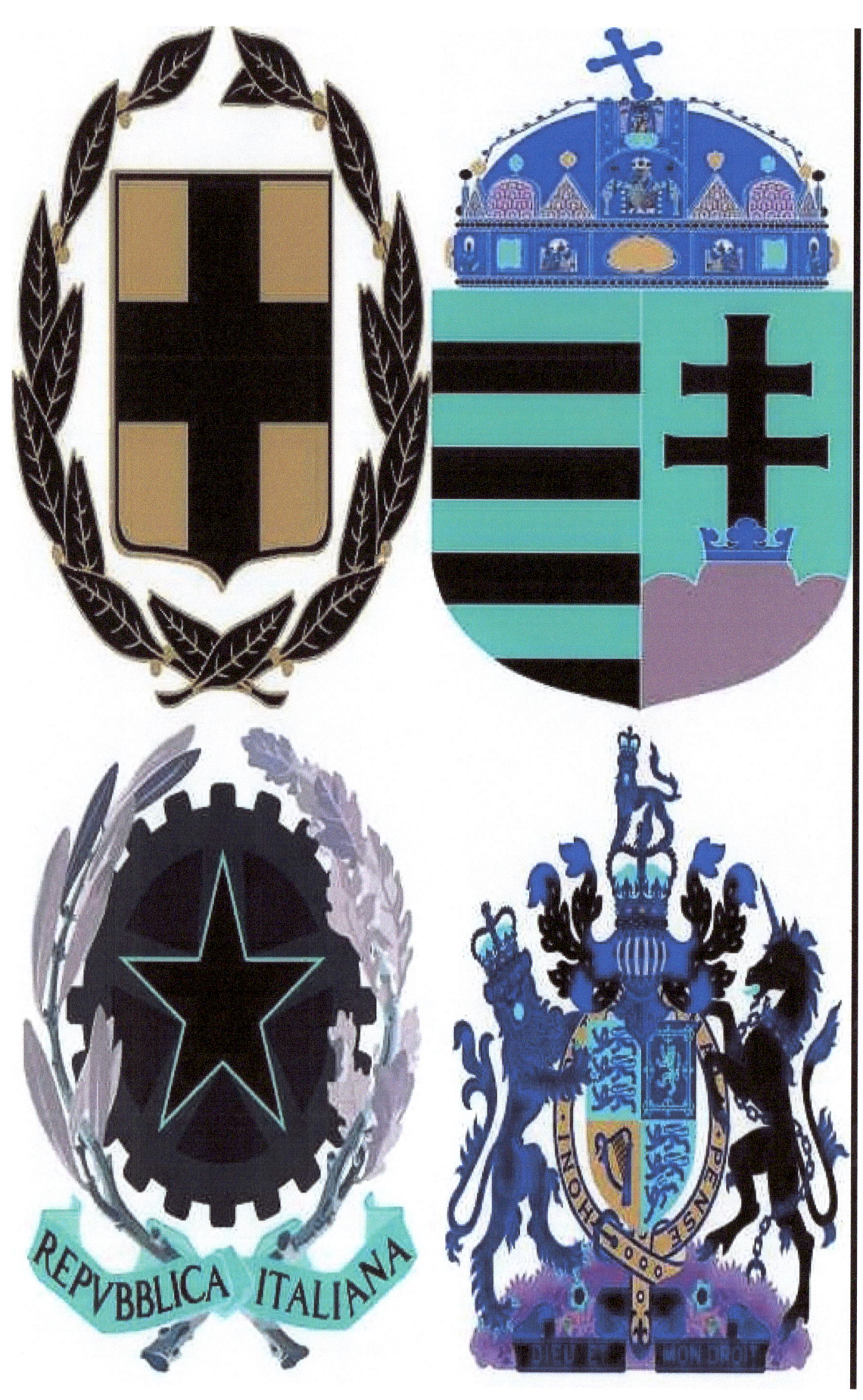

Arya Bàhram

Our Europe

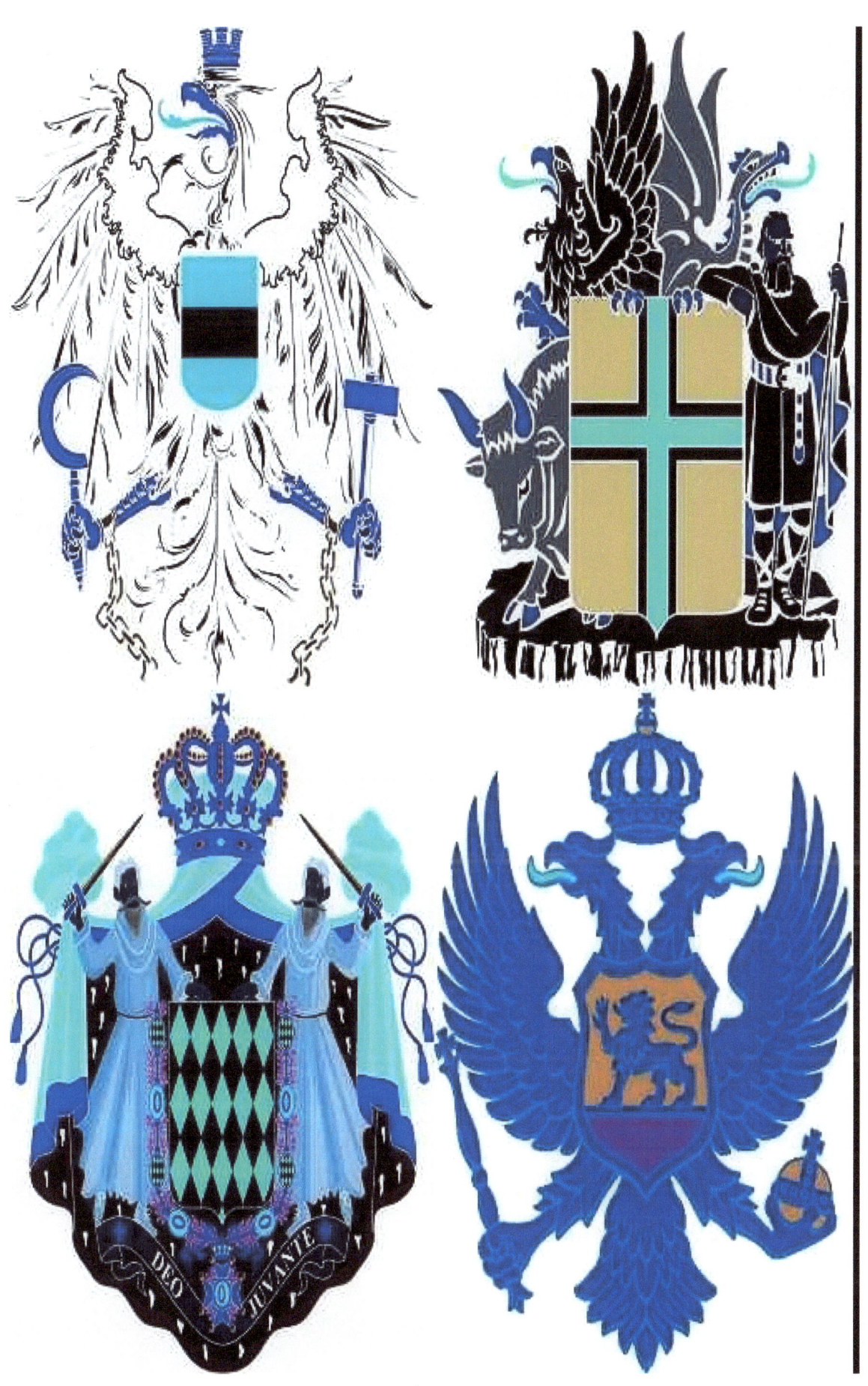

Arya Bàhram

Our Europe

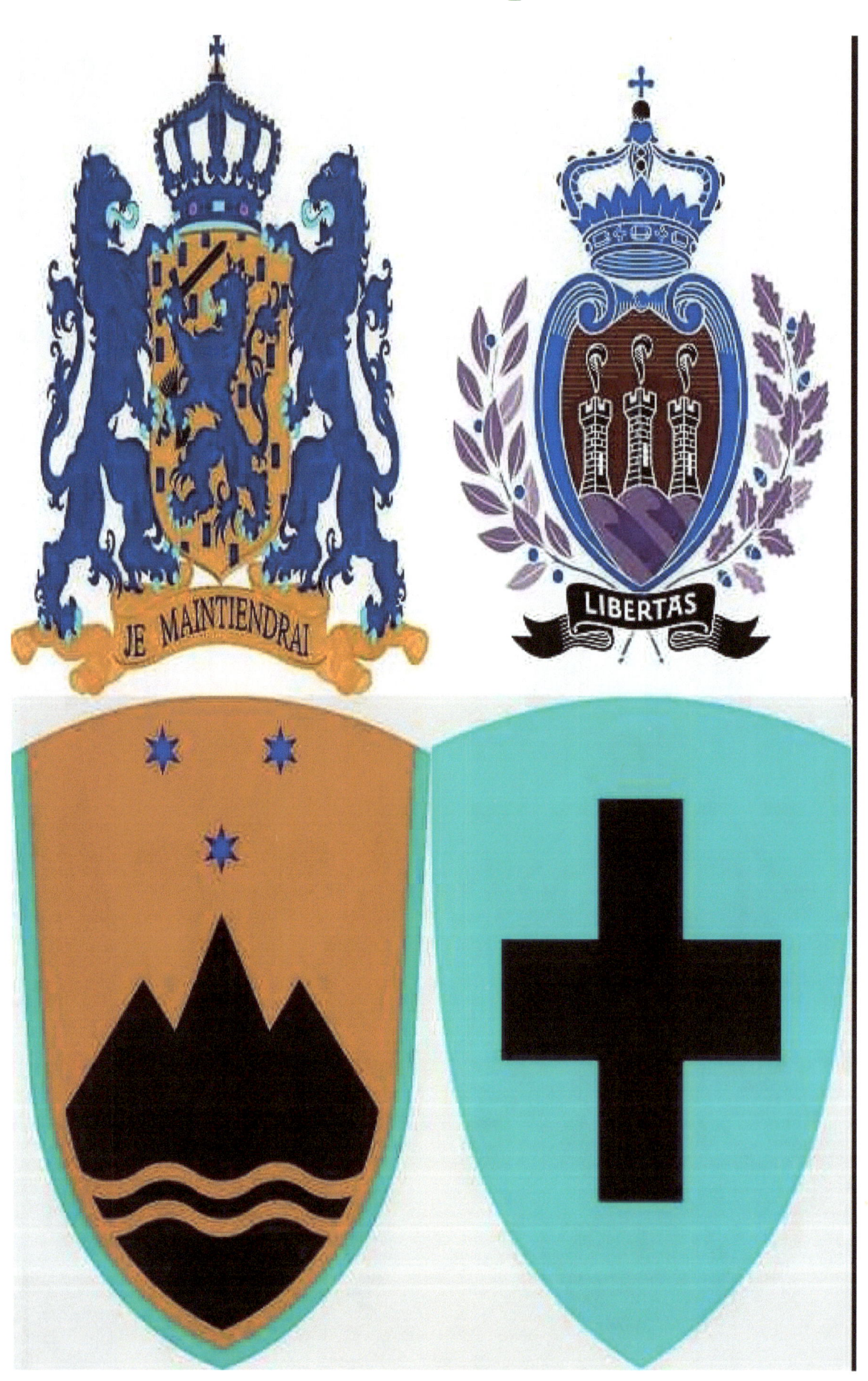

Arya Bàhram

Our Europe

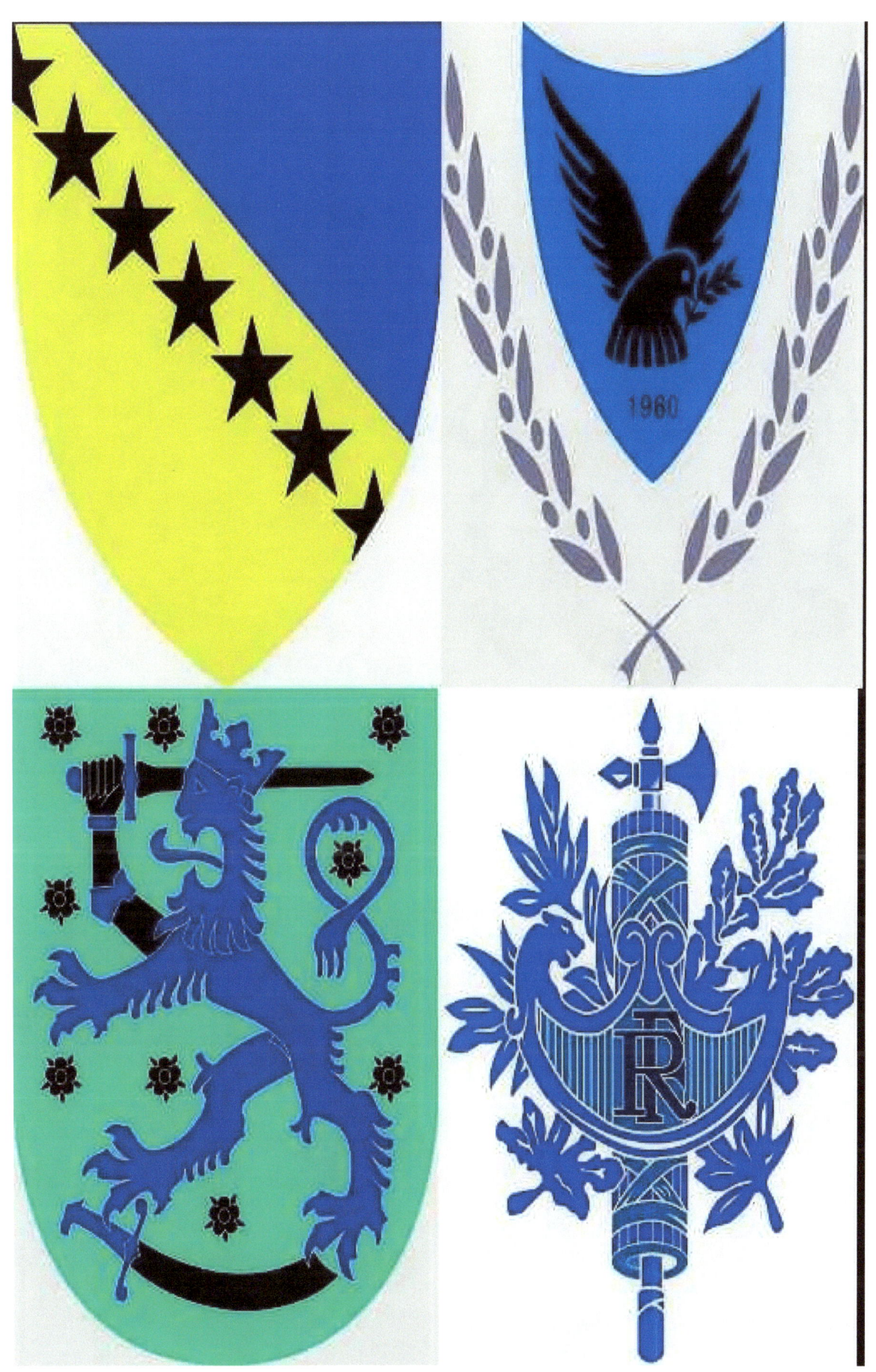

Arya Bàhram

Our Europe

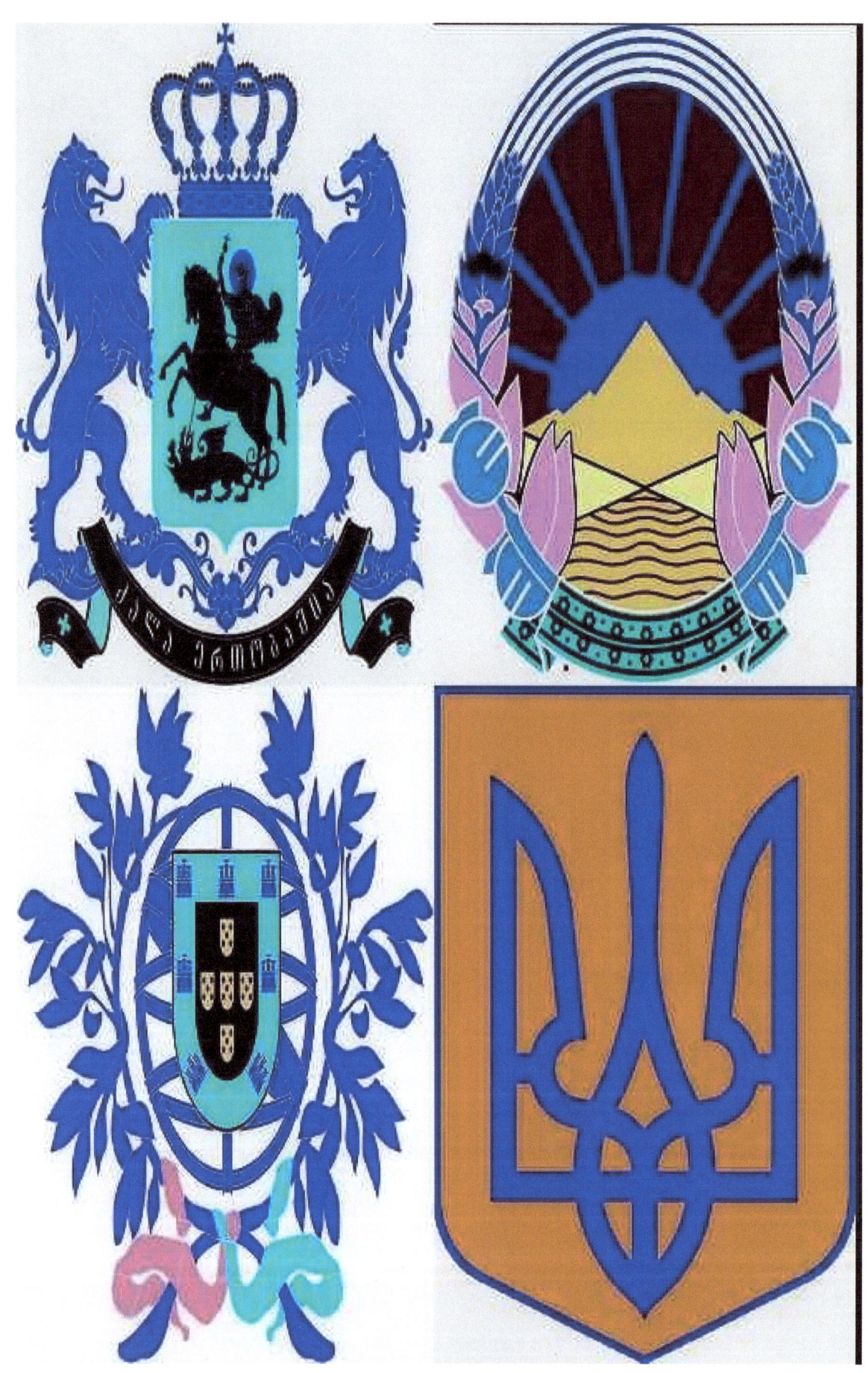

Arya Bàhram

Our Europe

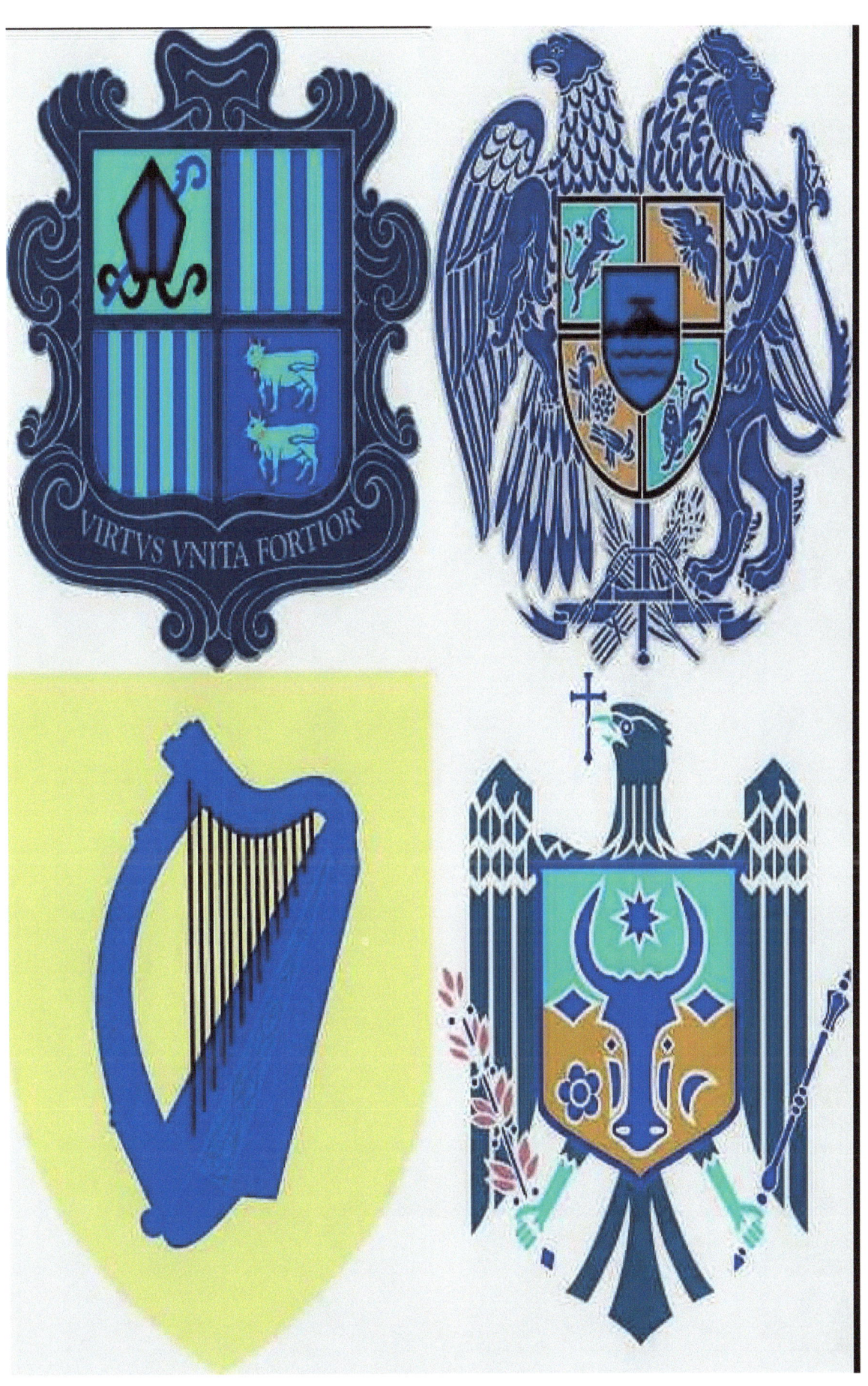

Arya Bàhram

Our Europe

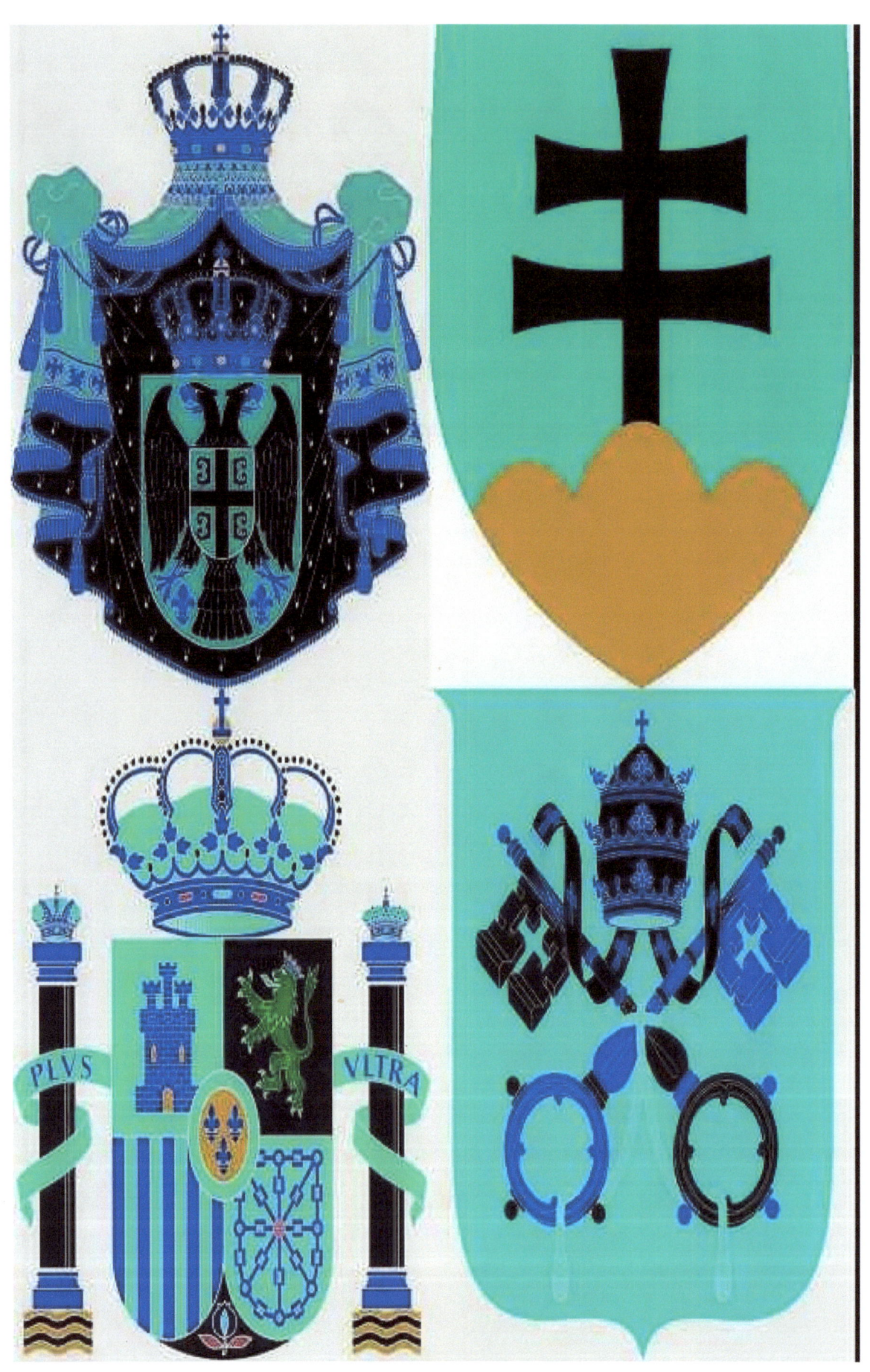

Arya Bàhram

Our Europe

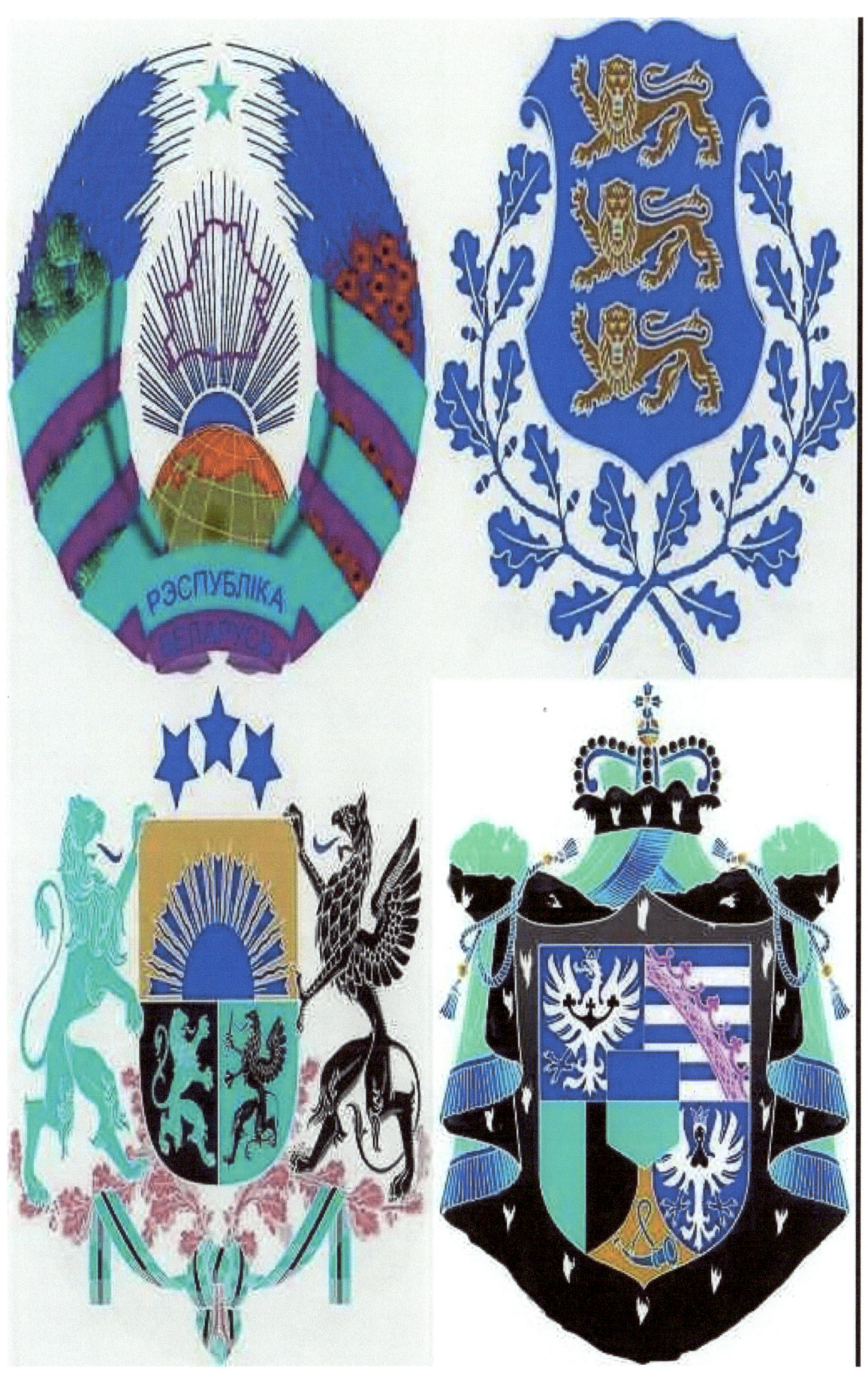

Arya Bàhram

Our Europe

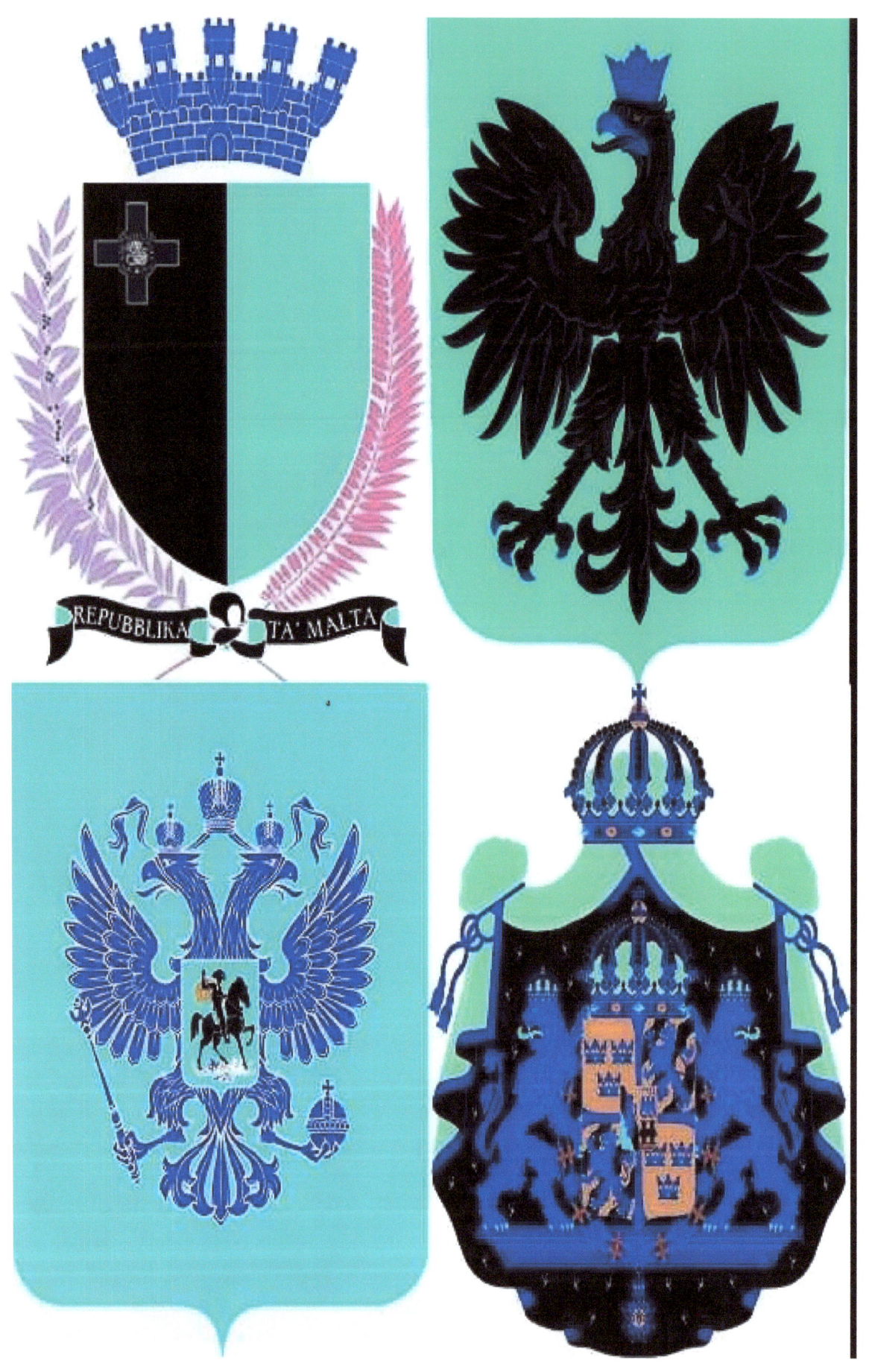

Arya Bàhram

Our Europe

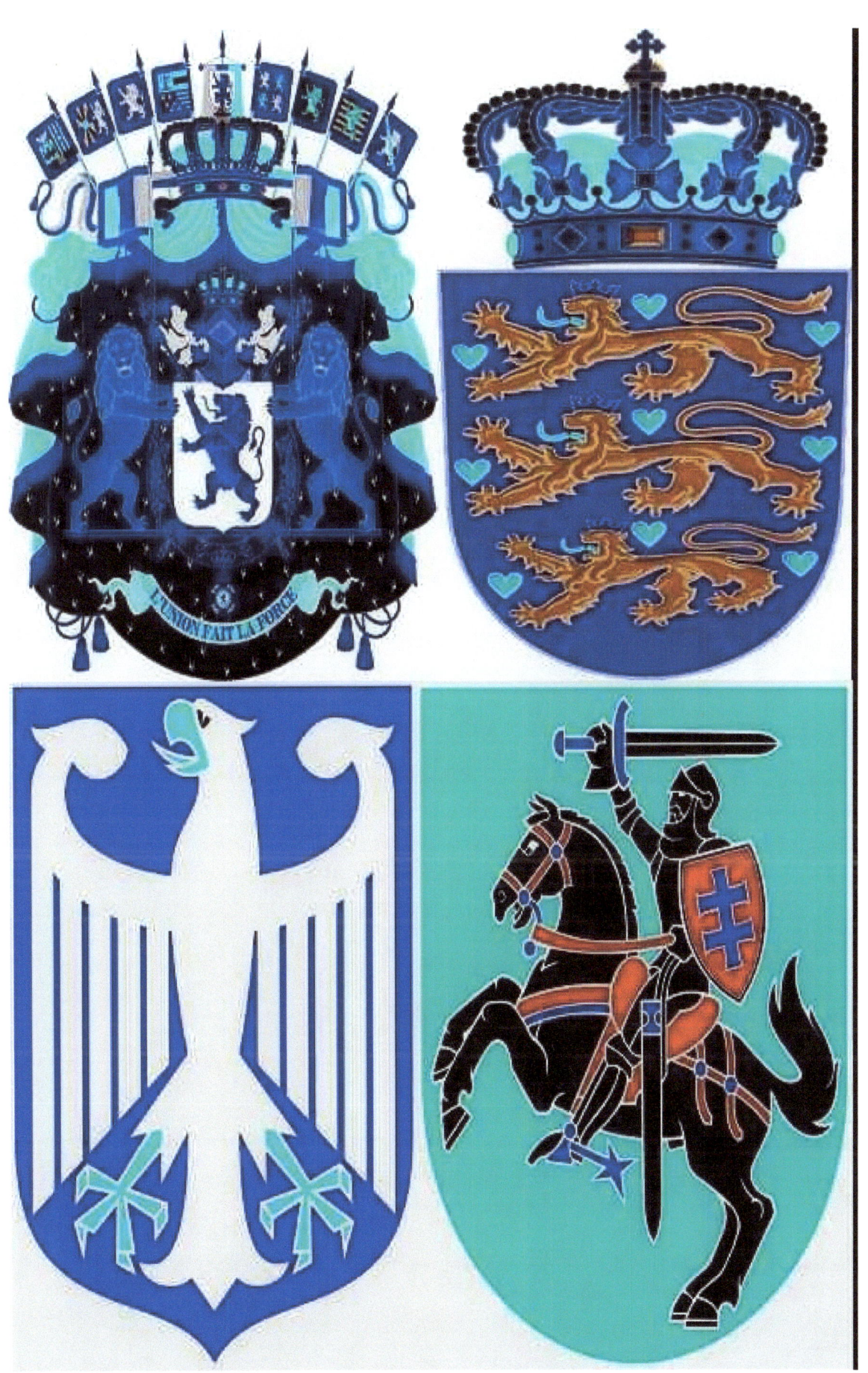

Arya Bàhram

Our Europe

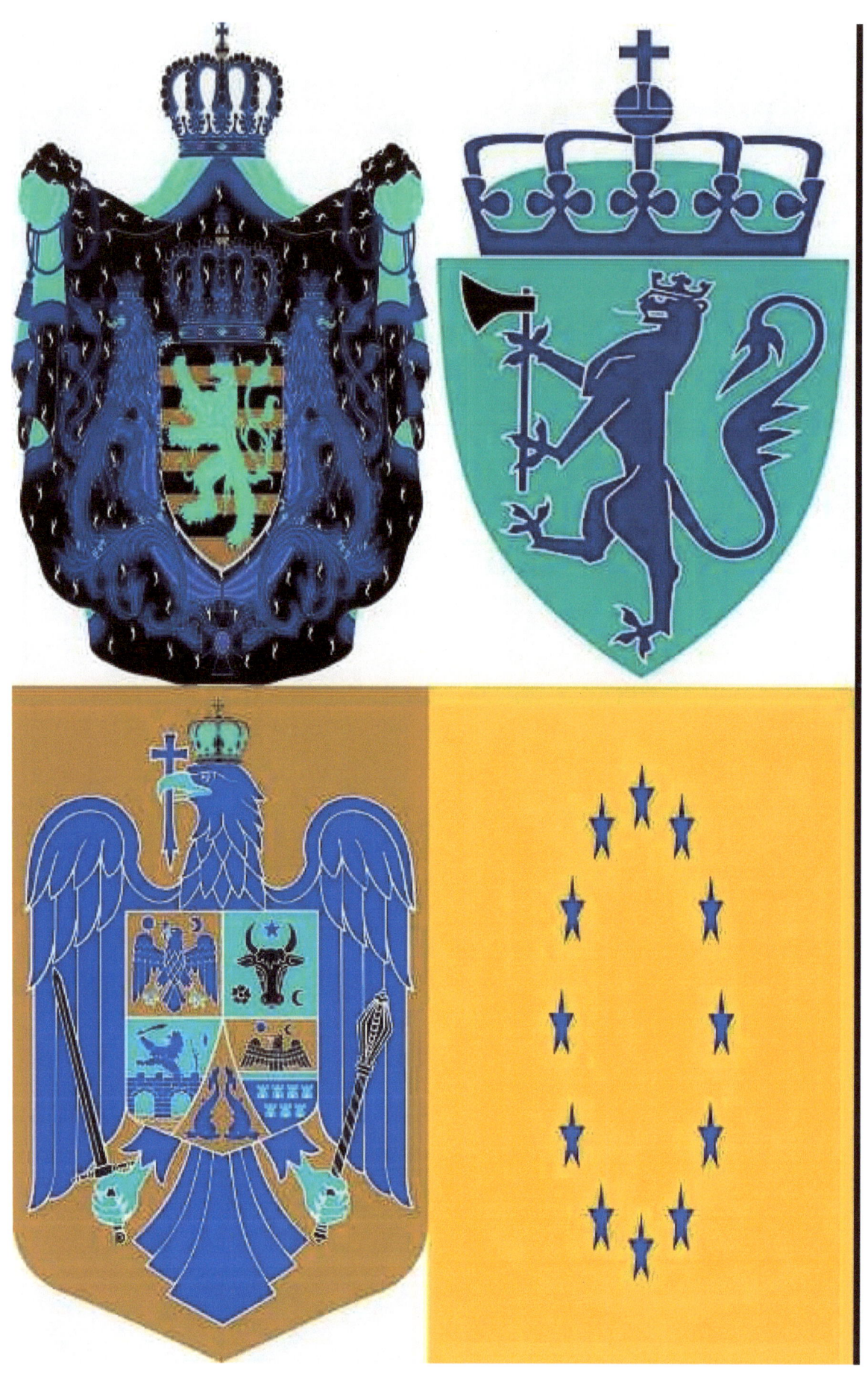

Arya Bàhram

Our Europe

Arya Bàhram